FEELING LIKE A KID

FEELING LIKE A KID

Childhood and Children's Literature

JERRY GRISWOLD

THE JOHNS HOPKINS UNIVERSITY PRESS

BALTIMORE

Johns Hopkins Paperback edition, 2022

2 4 6 8 9 7 5 3 1

Johns Hopkins University Press
2715 North Charles Street
Baltimore, Maryland 21218
www.press.jhu.edu

The Library of Congress has cataloged the hardcover edition of this book as follows:

Griswold, Jerome.
Feeling like a kid: childhood and children's literature / Jerry Griswold.
p. cm.
Includes bibliographical references (p.   ) and index.
ISBN 0-8018-8517-5 (acid-free paper)
1. Children's literature—History and criticism.
2. Children's literature—Themes, motives.
I. Title.
PN1009.A1G75 2006
809'.89282—DC22
2006007081

A catalog record for this book is available from the British Library.

ISBN 978-1-4214-4680-6 (Paperback)

Frontispiece. "Its Walls Were as of Jasper." Kenneth Grahame, *Dream Days* (Bodley Head, 1902). Illustration by Maxfield Parrish.

*Special discounts are available for bulk purchases of this book.
For more information, please contact Special Sales at specialsales@jh.edu.*

Pages 147–48 constitute an extension of this copyright page.

For my son, Colin Rodríguez Griswold
(1979–2005)

Contents

FEELING LIKE A KID

There should therefore be a time in adult life
devoted to revisiting the most important books of our youth.
Even if the books have remained the same, . . .
we have most certainly changed,
and our encounter with them will be a new thing.

—Italo Calvino, *The Uses of Literature*

INTRODUCTION

Five themes recur in classic and popular works of Children's Literature.

Snugness. Children like to play underneath tables or make tents from blankets and chairs; this is an activity common among the young but no longer seen in adulthood. That same sought-after pleasure also appears in children's books in their frequent and pleasing visions of the snug place—for example, grandfather's alpine cabin in *Heidi,* the Little House on the Prairie, and Badger's cozy underground home in *The Wind in the Willows.*

Scariness. From the very earliest age, when adults play the game of "Boo!" with infants, the young learn the surprising fact that

I

scariness can be discomforting fun. The world of Children's Literature is not the sunny and trouble-free place that grown-ups often remember it to be. Instead, it is a frightening realm where witches lure children, a wolf chats up Little Red Riding Hood, Mr. McGregor hunts Peter Rabbit, Max encounters the Wild Things, and Voldemort stalks Harry Potter.

Smallness. Moving miniature figurines around on the rug, fascinated by toy worlds, tiny tots love tiny people. In a similar way, in children's books—where Stuart Little drives around a miniature car or societies of insectlike creatures go about their parallel lives—issues of size are important and play a much larger role than they ever do in adult books.

Lightness. Compared to grown-ups, kids frequently seem light-hearted and lithe, while adults are more solid and serious and weighed down by responsibilities. It may not be surprising, then, that one of the unique features of Children's Literature is that airborne characters (from Peter Pan to Mary Poppins) abound.

Aliveness. Perhaps most obviously, Children's Literature differs from adult fare in the more frequent appearance of talking animals (for example, in *Doctor Dolittle*), living toys (as in *Pinocchio*), and animations of nature (the Man in the Moon and My Shadow). For the young, the whole universe is alive and full of companions.

These five themes or qualities in literature, looked at in a different way, can be seen as feelings or sensations prevalent in childhood.

Alison Lurie has identified a curious feature about those who write for the young. "The most gifted authors for children are not like other writers," Lurie says in her *Boys and Girls Forever*, because in some essential way they have remained in touch with their childhoods. Seconding that idea, critic Hugh Walpole observed that truly inspired writing for children is difficult because "it can only be done by somebody having a great deal of the child to his outlook and sensibilities."

That seems to be the case. When an interviewer asked famed picture-book artist Maurice Sendak how a childless author like himself could so sympathetically understand the young, Sendak mentioned his own intensely vivid memories of childhood: "I *was* a child," he pointedly said. When I asked Pamela Travers why her Mary Poppins books especially appealed to the young, she told me: "I have not forgotten my childhood. I can, as it were, turn aside and consult it."

These acute memories may be the most distinguishing feature of gifted writers for the young. Even in his eighties, writing his autobiography, children's poet and novelist John Masefield could remember an idiosyncrasy others may recall from their own childhoods: how, when he was young, he paid attention to things close at hand and could stare for hours into his box of toys and marbles.

Because they are still connected to their childhoods and sympathetic, then, the best writers for children can speak to the young. Looked at from the opposite direction, from the point of view of the young, this is the very source of their appeal; in preferring certain authors and works, while ignoring many others, the young confirm that there are a chosen few who can speak to them where they are. Simply said, the great writers for children know—and their stories speak of and reveal—what it feels like to be a kid.

SNUGNESS

Kids get a special pleasure from playing underneath tables, and setting up housekeeping in tents made of blankets and chairs, and creating forts in large cardboard boxes, and passing time behind the furniture. Adults are not immune to this delight; the daydream of retreating to a mountain cabin or the special satisfaction grown-ups take in outfitting a recreational vehicle with clever fittings, for example, comes close. Still, snugness seems a pleasurable feeling especially sought in childhood. We don't see adults playing under tables.

Since children seek this feeling, it isn't surprising that visions of the snug place abound in Children's Literature. It is the cozy underground home of Badger in *The Wind in the Willows*, where the wet and woebegone Rat and Mole find a fire-warmed shelter after having been lost in a winter storm. It is the underground hole to which Peter Rabbit retreats after his frightening misadventures in the wide world with Mr. McGregor, the place where he can climb into bed and his mother brings him camomile tea. It is all those sleeping places where children are comfy in their beds, like Heidi sleeping in her hay-filled nest in the attic of her grandfather's alpine hut. It is the space underneath the table, the tent made of blankets and chairs, the Little House on the prairie, the treehouse, the fort, the stockade, the cave, and other bastions of security and comfort.

There may be no better example of the pleasures of snugness than a moment found in *The Wind in the Willows*. Mole and Rat have passed the night snowbound and lost in the Wild Wood. Damp and cold, at their wits' end, they fortunately happen upon the entrance to Badger's underground home. These two shivering creatures feel rescued when Badger opens the door and welcomes them into his warm, underground abode with its crackling fire and comfy accommodations: "The two animals tumbled over each other to get inside, and heard the door shut behind them with joy and relief." As this begins to suggest, the snug place is a refuge and haven associated with sensations of comfort and security, with ease and well-being.

Kenneth Grahame, *The Wind in the Willows*
(1908; reprinted Holt, Rinehart & Winston, 1980).
Illustration by Michael Hague. © 1980 by Ariel Inc.

Maurice Sendak, *Where the Wild Things Are* (Harper & Row, 1963).
© 1963 by Maurice Sendak.

In fact, the snug place in children's stories has certain identifiable features. If we were to imagine an essay about such cozy childhood locales in a magazine like *Architectural Digest*, we might encounter a list that would tell us the attributes of the snug place.

Enclosed. When Mole and Rat rang Badger's bell, they heard the shuffling of slippers "approaching the door from the *inside*"; after the two creatures entered this home, they "heard the door shut *behind* them." Snugness, in other words, is a feature in a world where the dialectic of "inside" and "outside" is operative. Mole and Rat pass through a door and enter into enclosed space, a boundaried or circumscribed place.

Tight. The pleasures children take in womblike enclosures (under the table, behind the couch, in a tent made of blankets, and in a playhouse constructed from a large cardboard box) indicate how snugness is also associated with tight spaces. This is true in the shut-in nature of Badger's underground home. That sense of constricted space may be made even more acute by isolation and remoteness—in Randall Jarrell's *The Animal Family*, the Robinson Crusoe–like characters occupy a cabin circumscribed by an island; in Johanna Spyri's *Heidi*, grandfather's solitary hut seems more contracted because it is perched all alone on a mountain and surrounded by vast, uninhabited tracts and other mountains.

Small. Related to the sensation of enclosure are issues of size. The snug place is smaller. Laura Ingalls Wilder called her book *"Little House on the Prairie."* The miniature house that Peter Pan and the Lost Boys construct for Wendy arises from her request: "I wish I had a pretty house, the littlest ever seen." Beatrix Potter's genial spaces are also scaled-down locales where tiny animals carry on their lives behind the walls and where, in *The Tale of Two Bad Mice*, two creatures set up housekeeping in a dollhouse.

Simple. What lies behind this miniaturization and the vision of enclosed space is a wish to make life more manageable, a wish for control. Just as part of the pleasure of traveling is having fewer possessions to attend to, part of the pleasure of the snug place is that it is simple. Badger's underground home is not extravagant; instead, it is a locale where friends of "simple tastes" can be comfortable and where Badger has finished a "plain but ample supper." Hovering about this abode, in other words, is a comfortable modesty, a felicitous poverty. The hut in Spyri's novel is likewise warm and humble; Heidi and her grandfather have a simple diet of bread and cheese and milk, and their home is a place of so few possessions that, when Heidi comes to stay, her grandfather has to build her a chair. Theirs is an admirable frugality. Their wants few Their wishes all confined.

Well designed. Besides the manageability that arises from having few possessions, there is also a sense that the enclosed space is made shipshape by the thoughtful arrangement of objects. When Clara's grandmother comes to visit Heidi at her grandfather's alpine hut, she expresses an admiration "for the orderliness and cunning arrangement of the place." A similar scene occurs in *The Wind in the Willows* when Rat visits Mole's own underground home. While Mole apologizes for the sparseness of his furnishings, Rat enthuses about the clever features of his host's abode in terms that the owners of recreational vehicles often expect from their inspecting visitors: "What a capital little house this is!" Rat says cheerily. "So compact! So well planned! Everything here and everything in its place! . . . So this is the parlour? Splendid! Your own idea, those little sleeping-bunks in the wall? Capital!"

Remote. Snugness is also present in protected space. At one point in Grahame's novel, Mole compliments Badger on the subterranean home he has created:

[Mole] took the opportunity to tell Badger how comfortable and home-like it all felt to him. "Once well underground," he said, "you know exactly where you are. Nothing can happen to you, and nothing can get at you. You're entirely your own master, and you don't have to consult anybody or mind what they say. Things go on all the same overhead, and you let 'em, and don't bother about 'em. When you want to, up you go, and there the things are, waiting for you."

The Badger simply beamed on him. "That's exactly what I say," he replied. "There's no security, or peace and tranquillity, except under-ground. . . . No remarks passed on you by fellows looking over your wall, and, above all, no weather. . . . No, up and out of doors is good enough to roam about and get one's living in; but underground to come back to at last—that's my idea of home."

Safe. In his praise of underground homes, Mole emphasizes that "nothing can get at you." The snug place is a refuge. It is, for example, a shelter from threatening weather: grandfather's hut buffeted by threatening winds in *Heidi* or Badger's underground retreat in the midst of a snowstorm. But it may also be a refuge from others: a brick house into which three pigs retreat from the wolf, a room in which Anne Frank hides. Or it may simply offer immunity from the cares of the world; going under-ground, Mole says, "things go on all the same overhead, and you let 'em, and don't bother about 'em."

Guarded. Seen from an alternate point of view, the snug place serves not so much as a protection from encroaching outside threats but as a locale that is actively protected and defended from the inside. It is a guarded setting, and the impression of snugness appears in imagery of the fortress or, say, the stockade in *Treasure Island.*

Self-sufficient. Related to guardedness is the vision of the self-sufficient place. Like Robinson Crusoe who brings his necessities and comforts inside his fort and then pulls up the ladder after him, like children who provision their treehouses in the same way, Badger is surrounded by his winter stores. In his kitchen are bundles of herbs and nets of onions, eggs in baskets and hams hanging from the rafters; later we are told of Badger's rooms, half full of "piles of apples, turnips, and potatoes, baskets full of nuts, and jars of honey." Snug in his underground home, the hibernating Badger is provisioned and free from want.

Owned. The security of the guarded place is also associated with private property. In this way, the child's retreat to a tent of blankets or a position under the table can be seen as an active assertion of *me* and *mine.* For Freud, the initial state of the infant is an "oceanic" experience, where the self is not discriminated from the non-self. With ego formation and maturation come the construction of boundaries and a separation of infant from mother, inside from outside, internal from external. With every use of the words "No!" and "Mine!" likewise comes a healthy assertion of privacy and private property, a declaration of the self fortified and snug behind defense mechanisms. Playing alone, engaging in solitary games in private enclosures, the child rehearses individuality.

Hidden. The pleasure of ownership is also an explanation of the association of snugness with hidden and secret places. The child who retreats to his or her private place is engaged in a geographic or architectural assertion of individuality; keeping secrets, from which parents and others are excluded, is likewise an assertion of individuality. This is exactly what occurs in Frances Hodgson Burnett's *The Secret Garden*. For Burnett's young characters, the great value of the walled and enclosed garden is that it is their secret, which they can keep from adults until they choose to extend membership.

Psychologists would say that the desire to find pleasure in small, enclosed, and tight spaces amounts to an attempt to recapture the security of the womb. But there is more to it than that. By pulling themselves up by their own bootstraps, by asserting individuality and drawing their own boundaries, the young find in the snug place that wonderful combination of the reassuringly familiar and personal assertiveness: a womb of one's own.

Cozy Times

Turning from space to time, we can note that certain occasions are especially apt for an evocation of snugness. Mole and Rat, for example, are driven to Badger's cozy home by a winter storm and find there a refuge where they can warm and dry themselves, relax and rest. Meteorologically speaking, the best condition for an evocation of snugness is stormy weather. Horrific storms, like those that assault grandfather's alpine home in *Heidi*, demarcate even more dramatically the hostility of the universe in contrast to the snugness of the shelter. Even mildly inclement weather, like that of the British Isles, can provide an occasion for a vision of indoor coziness. In the closing words of *The Voyages of Dr. Dolittle*, Hugh Lofting's character returns at long last to his home and invites his guests inside on a drizzly day: "You know, there's something rather attractive in the bad weather of England—when you've got a kitchen fire to look forward to. . . . Four o'clock! Come along—we'll just be in time for a nice tea."

Besides stormy weather, seasonally the best time for an evocation of snugness is winter, especially after snow has fallen. The heightened contrast—between the cold outdoors and the warmth indoors, between the monochromes of a snow-covered world outside and a colorful vividness inside—sharpens boundaries and assigns value to the cozy haven.

In the northern hemisphere, at least, one of the best dates on the calendar for an evocation of snugness is Christmas. Perhaps the most touching moment in Louisa May Alcott's *Little Women* is created when father comes home from the war, steps out of winter's cold and damp, closes the door behind him, and reunites with his wife and four daughters around the fire on Christmas Day. Indeed, Mole and Rat's visit to Badger's home takes place during this holiday season.

But more than any other occasion, nighttime and bedtime are especially apt times for visions of snugness. When Heidi comes to live in her grandfather's hut, he allows her to choose where she will sleep during her stay. Investigating various places, Heidi finally climbs into the attic, assembles a cozy nest for herself from the hay, covers it with a sheet, and retires at night to slumber there. Then follows a universally familiar and touching scene that might be called the Tableau of the Sleeping Child. Grandfather, worried that Heidi might be frightened on her

Johanna Spyri, *Heidi* (Houghton Mifflin, 1923).
Illustration by Gustaf Tenggren.

Chris Van Allsburg, *The Garden of Abdul Gasazi*
(Houghton Mifflin, 1979). © 1979 by Chris Van Allsburg.

first night in the Alps, checks on her: "He mounted the ladder and went and stood by the child's bed. . . . Just now the moonlight was falling through the round window straight on to Heidi's bed. She lay under the heavy coverlet, her cheeks rosy with sleep, her head peacefully resting on her little round arm, and with a happy expression on her baby face as if dreaming of something pleasant."

In the middle of Spyri's book, however, Heidi is taken from her grandfather and sent to live with strangers in Frankfurt. Not feeling at home in the Sesemanns' mansion and besieged by the tyrannical governess Miss Rottenmeier, Heidi feels more like a bird in a cage than a bird in its nest. She grows homesick and ill. Her distress is revealed by a sleep disorder: she begins to sleepwalk, always opening the door of the mansion she longs to escape. Fortunately, the family physician is adept with psychological problems and prescribes a remedy for her disease and somnambulism: Heidi is to be sent back to the Alps.

Heidi's reunion with her grandfather is the most touching scene in the book. This homecoming is also a return to snugness and sound sleep.

Later when Heidi went indoors, she found her bed already made up for her; the hay had been piled high for it and smelt deliciously, for it had only just been got in, and her grandfather had carefully spread and tucked in the clean sheets. It was with a happy heart that Heidi lay down in it that night, and her sleep was sounder than it had been all the time she was away. Her grandfather got up at least ten times during the night and mounted the ladder to see if Heidi was all right.... But Heidi did not stir. She slept soundly all night long because the great burning and longing of her heart was at last satisfied.

Perhaps this connection between snugness and sleeping is obvious. Restful sleep, and even the light somnolence of napping, requires conditions of ease and security, a comfort absent of potential threats, a well-being in which one is able to relax. Even a dog will not curl up and slumber if these conditions are lacking. And these conditions for sleep—serenity, safety, agreeableness—amount to a description of snugness. A snug place, we might say, is a place where one can sleep or nap.

All these temporal conditions—winter and Christmas, nighttime and bedtime, sleeping and dreaming—come together in Clement Moore's well-known poem "A Visit from St. Nicholas," where, under "the moon on the breast of the new fallen snow," Santa's arrival is imminent.

> 'Twas the night before Christmas, when all through the house
> Not a creature was stirring, not even a mouse.
> The stockings were hung by the chimney with care,
> In hopes that St. Nicholas soon would be there;

Clement C. Moore, *The Night before Christmas* (Scholastic, 1985).
Illustration by James Marshall. © 1985 by James Marshall.

The children were nestled all snug in their beds,
While visions of sugarplums danced in their heads.

Here, again, is the Tableau of the Sleeping Child (or children) seen in *Heidi* when grandfather looks in on the little girl so cozy in her attic nest and "dreaming of something pleasant." Here, too, "visions of sugarplums" dance in the heads of dreaming children "nestled all snug in their beds."

A Shelter for Daydreaming

In his now famous studies, Canadian neurologist Wilder Penfield showed that humans have a biological need to dream. Penfield designed an experiment in which his research subjects were permitted to sleep but were prevented from dreaming by being awakened just at the moment they began to exhibit the first signs of dreaming (signaled by rapid eye movement, or REM, sleep). When denied the chance to dream, Penfield's research subjects became unhealthy, confused, and psychotic. Indeed, although Penfield had planned to conduct his experiment for a month, he was obliged to break it off after only a week because his subjects began to exhibit bizarre behavior that endangered them.

Since humans have a need to dream, we might consider just what it is we need to do. As any thoughtful person will have noticed, dreaming involves organizing the miscellaneous experiences of our waking lives into *stories*, into imagery and coherent narratives that (more or less) make sense of our lives. If troubled by the greediness of a companion, for example, we may dream of a dragon guarding a treasure chest; if worried about situations of potential embarrassment, we may dream about being naked. In that sense, everyone at night is a creative writer. And in that way, the dream story brings together the abundant and varied experiences of our waking life and makes them more connected and orderly.

James Barrie talks about this phenomenon in the opening of his *Peter Pan*. The daytime lives of children, he observes, are full of varied and miscellaneous events: the "first day at school, religion, fathers, the round pond, needle-work, murders, hangings, verbs that take the dative, chocolate pudding day, . . . pulling out your tooth yourself, and so on." To make sense of these and of life, the young need to dream at night, assembling that miscellany into a unified narrative, a parallel story full of dreamy analogues. By way of example, Barrie suggests that these varied daytime experiences might come together in the form of a dream about "coral reefs and rakish-looking craft in the offing, and savages and lonely lairs, and gnomes who are mostly tailors, and caves through which a river runs, and princes with six elder brothers, and a hut fast going to decay, and one very small old lady with a hooked nose."

But we can go further and say that the biological need for dreaming revealed by Penfield's experiments is also evident in that activity known as daydreaming. Barrie himself makes this link when he suggests that the kind of story making occurring in dreams at night also occurs when—and here he uses an image that has become important in this chapter—the young play in tents made "with the chairs and table-cloth."

Children need to daydream. It's not that grown-ups don't have the same need and never daydream or drift away in reverie. They do. But as the behavior of the young suggests, children need to daydream more. The young not only play under tables, they move tiny figurines around on the rug, varoom around the house like a motorcycle, talk to their teddy bears, arrange tea parties for dolls, gallop on stick horses, and sing songs to imaginary friends. This is only the beginning of a catalog of kinds of imaginative play and states of reverie present in childhood. These examples are offered only to suggest that the young need to daydream—engage in wakeful story making—more than grown-ups do. We don't hear of business executives, for example, whose job descriptions permit them two hours a day to move tiny action figures around on their desktops.

There is, then, a connection between snugness and daydreaming. In his masterful study *The Poetics of Space*, Gaston Bachelard mentions how the home may be a shelter for dreaming; we can go further and say that, for the young, the snug place is a shelter for daydreaming. In the same way that we need protected and comfortable conditions in which to sleep and dream, the young need secure and cozy locales in which they can create and enact make-believe stories that meet their needs and make their lives understandable. The snug place is a special venue where the fantasizing youngster can engage in this needed story making in peace.

When children crawl under tables or into tents made of chairs and the tablecloth, they enter dreamhouses. In this sense, every snug place is Plato's cave of ideas. Here is an explanation of why the snug place is especially prized in childhood and so conspicuous in Children's Literature.

Felicitous Space

Of course, one child's coziness may be another child's claustrophobia. Images of the opposite of snugness also appear in children's stories: the confining belly of the whale for Pinocchio and Geppetto, the jail-like Gingerbread House in which the witch imprisons Hansel and Gretel, the oppressive mansion in

Frankfurt that nature-girl Heidi wishes to escape. We find an example in *The Wind in the Willows:* while Badger and Mole (both underground creatures) wax enthusiastic about the comforts of subterranean sanctuaries, Rat (an aboveground animal who always sleeps with the window open) grows restless in Badger's underground home and is eager to depart those stifling circumstances.

Instead of wishing for snugness, some literary children want the opposite and are eager to be out and doing. Plucky Jim Hawkins in *Treasure Island* feels oppressed when the pirates trap him in his home at the Benbow Inn, and a sense of claustrophobia overwhelms him when he hides in an apple barrel and overhears the buccaneers plotting; he feels right only when he has left his shipboard confinement and escaped to the island, where he can explore and roam freely. Tom Sawyer also feels beleaguered when he is trapped in McDougal's Cave or confined to home by Aunt Polly; he feels right only when he is abroad and playing hooky, especially when escaping such chores as whitewashing the fence. While one child seeks a sheltering snugness, another wants the freedom of the open air and says, "Don't fence me in."

A child's sense of security determines whether enclosed space is perceived as reassuring and desirable or confining and abhorrent. In *Childhood and Society*, Erik Erickson identifies as the first and most fundamental stage of childhood the development of the feeling of "basic trust," an existential confidence that the world is more or less all right. When basic trust is missing, the child experiences life as unpredictable and full of jeopardy. And when this insecurity is framed in spatial terms, the world seems a terrifyingly vast place in which the child has no anchor.

Here is how Laura Ingalls finds life and the Kansas Territory before her pioneer family builds their home in *Little House on the Prairie:*

Kansas was an endless flat land. . . . Day after day they traveled in [their covered wagon], and saw nothing but the rippling grass and the enormous sky. In a perfect circle the sky curved to the level land, and the wagon was in the circle's exact middle. . . . They couldn't get out of the middle of that circle. . . . [At night] the camp fire was small and lost in so much space. . . . Next day the land was the same, the sky was the same, the circle did not change. . . . Far away on the prairie the wolves howled.

In this vast and indifferent universe, Laura feels vulnerable: "All around them there was nothing but grassy prairie spreading to the edge of the sky. . . . The land and the sky seemed too large, and Laura felt small." The feeling here is the same as in Pascal's famous statement in his *Pensées*, when he was staring

Laura Ingalls Wilder, *Little House on the Prairie*
(Harper & Brothers, 1953). Illustration by Garth Williams.
© 1953, renewed 1981 by Garth Williams.

at the stars: "The silence of those eternal spaces terrifies me."

This absence of spatial security in a vastness, these same feelings of anxiety and vulnerability, appear in Russell Hoban's children's book *The Mouse and His Child* when the title characters find themselves in the midst of a war where animals are fighting over "territory." They ask what that is and are told:

"A territory is your place," said the drummer boy. "It's where everything smells right. It's where you know the runways and hideouts, night or day. It's what you fought for, or what your father fought for, and you feel all safe and strong there. It's the place where, when you fight, you win."

"That's your territory," said the fifer. "Somebody else's territory is something else again. That's where you feel all sick and scared and want to run away, and that's where the other side mostly wins."

This information troubles the mouse father: "What chance has anybody got without a territory?"

Properly understood, snugness is a remedy sought for the existential discomfort with expansiveness, and the snug place is an enclosed locale where that vulnerability is exchanged for feelings of comfort and security. When the Little House on the Prairie is at last constructed, Laura finally feels a sense of well-being: "It was nice to be living in a house again. . . . The fire merrily crackled, a fat duck roasted, and the cornbread baked. Everything was snug and cozy again. . . . Everything was all right."

The snug place, then, is a bastion of security and a safe anchorage where the soul's calmness can be restored and well-being enclosed. More importantly, from this safe center the feelings of basic trust and well-being can be extended to the world at large.

Bachelard links this well-being to the picture most frequently drawn by the very young, that picture sometimes called the "Happy House." It is a drawing of a square home whose squat proportions indicate that it is very much rooted in the world. It has a door, because this is a place of comings and goings; and it has a window, indicating an "inside" and an "outside." There is a chimney with lively smoke swirling out of this place that is clearly warm and inhabited. Often, too, the house is surrounded by tall and guarding trees and by happy and blooming flowers. Sometimes, at a height, sheltering mountains surround it and below a river of time passes along. And the sun? The sun shines happily on all of this.

SCARINESS

Adults, in my experience, don't like to have pointed out to them that childhood is a very scary time and the world of Children's Literature a very scary place. Forgetting their own childhoods, many grown-ups prefer a sentimental notion of childhood, where happy youngsters inhabit a trouble-free country and the sun is always shining. In a similar way, adults often have a saccharine notion of Children's Literature as sweet and cute, but to maintain that illusion they have to seize on happy and upbeat moments and race over events of the other kind.

Take Beatrix Potter's animal tales. The misty-eyed look adults get at the mention of these little books suggests they have forgotten the many anxious moments in the stories. When Peter Rabbit's mother explains why he is not to go into Mr.

McGregor's garden, she warns, "Your father had an accident there; he was put in a pie by Mrs. McGregor." Matter-of-fact, Potter does not pull any punches or shrink from the mention of death. Indeed, the story soon turns terrifying once Peter enters the forbidden garden: "Round the end of the cucumber frame, whom should he meet but Mr. McGregor!"

Rather than cute, if the truth be known, the world of Potter's books is really one of constant threats and vulnerability: where Tom Kitten is trussed up in a roly-poly pudding and about to become someone's dinner, where Jeremy Fisher is swallowed by a trout, where a fox has designs on Jemima Puddle-Duck, where an owl holds Squirrel Nutkin in his claws, and where a cat has captured Benjamin Bunny. But only an honest adult, ready to set aside sentimentality and reread her books, will notice the essential scariness of Beatrix Potter. Then passing time in her world seems less like a holiday in a summer cottage in the Lake District and more like a passage through some carnival House of Horrors.

Adults, it seems to me, remember what they wish. They melt in nostalgia at the mention of *The Story of Babar*. They forget that six sentences into that book Jean De Brunhoff introduces trauma: "Babar is riding on his mother's back when a wicked hunter, hidden by some bushes, shoots at them. The hunter has killed Babar's mother."

Beatrix Potter, *The Tale of Peter Rabbit* (Warne, 1902).

Or take Laura Ingalls Wilder's *Little House on the Prairie*. When I have asked people about their favorite childhood reading, I have noticed that most adult memories of Wilder's novel fasten on the image in the title, as if the happy hut of Heidi's grandfather had been transported from the Alps to Kansas's flatlands. But in truth, Wilder's book is a vision of constant precariousness at odds with the bliss adults recall: on their journey out west, the family's wagon narrowly escapes falling through thawing ice and later is nearly swept away by a raging river; building their house, Ma is injured by a falling log, and a neighbor is nearly asphyxiated when digging at the bottom of their well; on one occasion the cabin catches on fire, and on another it is threatened by a prairie wildfire; then the entire family falls gravely ill with fever while Indians are holding war councils to decide whether to attack the settlers; at night, a panther screams and wolves howl. In recalling *Little House on the Prairie*, a more representative image might be the one of Pa at the window with his gun in the middle of the night and the terrified family huddling together while a pack of wolves scratch at the door.

And as for scariness, what would a fairy tale be without it? Snow White harassed by an apple-bearing sorceress. Jack, once he ascends the beanstalk, threatened by the giant ogre. Little

Red Riding Hood encountering a leering wolf. Hansel and Gretel about to become a witch's dinner.

In fact, scariness seems to play a larger role in stories for children than in those for adults. For grown-ups, the frightening seems a specialty market; while some adults enjoy reading thrillers by authors like Stephen King, others read romance novels or detective stories or science fiction. For the young, however, fear seems so common as almost to be an omnipresent feature in their literature—where Voldemort stalks Harry Potter, Injun Joe pursues Tom Sawyer, Long John Silver conspires against Jim Hawkins, Mr. McGregor hunts Peter Rabbit, and fairy-tale stepmothers and witches harass girls and boys.

Of course, the young have a lower threshold for fear. It takes less to make tots tremble than to frighten grown-ups. Margaret Hamilton, playing the Wicked Witch in MGM's *The Wizard of Oz*, may make the young quake in their seats when she threatens Dorothy, "I'll get you my pretty, and your little dog too." But by the principle of neurasthenia—the numbness that comes from frequent stimulation—jaded adults require more intense horror, along the lines of Hannibal Lecter in *The Silence of the Lambs*, to even get their pulses racing.

What all this suggests is that fear is more acute in kids' lives than in the lives of grown-ups. It may be the terror of going to

Maurice Sendak, *Where the Wild Things Are* (Harper & Row, 1963).
© 1963 by Maurice Sendak.

bed alone in the dark. It may be the threatening sound of the vacuum cleaner or the sucking bathtub drain. It may be bullies in the schoolyard. It may be the one house in the neighborhood, occupied by an old woman or an old man, avoided by all the kids. Or it may be still other adults, ones they have been warned about, the ones who lie in wait to snatch them.

Children's lives are not all sweetness and light, despite what grown-ups would like to believe. Childhood has more than its measure of anxieties and fears—some big, some small—but children do not know which are "big" and which are "small." In his poem "Children Selecting Books in a Library," Randall Jarrell observes: "Their tales are full of sorcerers and ogres / Because their lives are."

The Good Scare

"The most famous children's book in the world," scholar Jack Zipes suggests, is Heinrich Hoffmann's *Struwwelpeter* (sometimes translated into English as Shock-headed Peter). While perhaps not so well known among Americans, this German book has produced millions of nightmares among European children since it was published in 1845, and it continues to terrify to this day.

The manifest purpose of Hoffmann's illustrated storybook is to frighten children into being good. The book's stories tell, for example, about Harriet who plays with matches and is burned up, and about Augustus who refuses to eat his soup and shrinks to sticklike proportions, only to die in five days. But the consensus is that the most frightening of these tales is "The Story of Little Suck-a-Thumb" where Conrad is warned by Mama about his offensive habit; but when her back is turned, he puts the digit in his mouth and the Scissor-man (a tailor) bursts through the door and snips off both the boy's thumbs. The last picture shows a chastened, bleeding, amputated Conrad.

"When I was a child, *Struwwelpeter* terrified me," Marina Warner wrote in a typical reminiscence about the book.

I did not find it funny because I sucked my thumb and I was truly afraid the tailor, drawn like a leaping pair of scissors, would come to get me and cut off my thumbs, as he does to little Suck-a-Thumb.... I must have been around seven when I read *Struwwelpeter*, and it took such possession of me that I kept going back and looking at the Scissor-man .. . until I could bear it no longer and took the book to my father when he was gardening and asked him to burn it on the bonfire.

A little more than a hundred years later, a different scary book came down the pike when Maurice Sendak published his now beloved *Where the Wild Things Are*. In the opening, Max is misbehaving and then finds himself in a land of monsters, the Wild Things, who seem as horrific as Hoffmann's Scissor-man: "They

Heinrich Hoffmann, *Der Struwwelpeter* (Rütten, 1845).

roared their terrible roars and gnashed their terrible teeth and rolled their terrible eyes and showed their terrible claws." But in the next scene, Sendak dramatically parts company from Hoffmann.

Sendak's Max is not intimidated like Hoffmann's thumbless Conrad. After the monsters do their best to terrify him, Max gives them a start and "tame[s] them with a magic trick of staring into all their yellow eyes without blinking once and they were frightened." Then, as the story continues, Max marshals these critters to do *his* bidding.

Between *Struwwelpeter* and *Where the Wild Things Are* might be seen two different traditions in the uses of scariness: one meant to intimidate children into being good and the other meant to encourage their mastery of fears. This distinction can be made clearer by considering two versions of a well-known fairy tale.

Charles Perrault's "Little Red Riding Hood" is a cautionary tale meant to teach a lesson. In this version of the familiar story, a young and innocent girl travels through the woods and meets the wily wolf. The wolf gets to grandma's before the child, consumes the old woman, and dons her clothes. Deceiving the girl, the wolf then pounces on Little Red Riding Hood and eats her up. And that's where Perrault's version of the story ends—except for his addition of a moral regarding the dangers of naiveté and advising young girls to learn that some men are not to be trusted. His story lacks the relief of a happy ending. Indeed, like *Struwwelpeter* and other cautionary tales, the child who hears Perrault's story is left to tremble and contemplate horrible consequences as a warning.

Perrault's abrupt conclusion seems to have troubled the Grimm Brothers because decades later, when they fashioned their own version of the story, "Little Red Cap," they considerably expanded the ending. In their rendition, the carnivore's slaughter of the innocents still occurs but then a hunter happens by, does a cesarian section (cutting open the wolf's belly and extricating the still-living grandma and girl), then fills the wolf's belly with rocks, and the villain runs off and dies. But even this punishment of the evildoer is not enough of a happy ending for the Grimms, and they continue further: Little Red Cap makes a second trip through the woods and meets another wolf; this time, however, she is not fooled and dashes on to grandma's where the two of them successfully conspire to kill the lupine villain.

Perrault's and the Grimms' versions of the same story reveal the two different traditions of intimidation and mastery. In Perrault, fear is inspired but unrelieved; written as an admonition

Penrhyn W. Coussens, *A Child's Book of Stories* (Duffield, 1911).
Illustration by Jessie Willcox Smith.

and lacking a happy ending, in a manner very much like *Struwwelpeter*, this scary story is meant to intimidate, and youngsters are expected to learn a lesson. Didactic in a different way, the Grimm Brothers' extended conclusion shows the girl's having learned the lesson that Perrault only appended to his abrupt ending; in their version's happy ending, fear is eventually relieved and the scare becomes a precipitating occasion for the model child to acquire and demonstrate mastery. Like Max, who trumps the monsters in *Where the Wild Things Are*, the Grimms' little heroine bests the beast.

Nowadays, the tradition of intimidation has fallen out of favor, and Hoffmann's story of thumbless Conrad and his other frightening tales strike us as either objectionable or old-fashioned; indeed, as I write this, a play based on *Struwwelpeter* ("Shockheaded Peter") is on Broadway, and Hoffmann's bizarre anecdotes that link child raising with bloodletting are played for laughs. If such laughter signals fears conquered, then here, too, is an explanation of the popularity of the "Lemony Snicket" books, with their over-the-top and bizarrely comic persecutions. In our own time, only the argument for mastery has been able to assemble a defense for scariness, against high-minded censors and overcautious parents who insist children should be given only sunny and harmless stories.

"Too scary for children" was, in fact, the criticism made by some experts on child raising when Sendak's *Where the Wild Things Are* was published in 1963. Later, when the book won the prestigious Caldecott Medal, Sendak directly faced his critics in his acceptance speech. First of all, he challenged their sentimental notion that childhood is a trouble-free time: "What is too often overlooked, is the fact that from their earliest years children live on familiar terms with disrupting emotions, that fear and anxiety are an intrinsic part of their everyday lives, that they continually cope with frustration as best they can." Then, mounting the argument for mastery and justifying his own book in terms of facing and conquering fears, Sendak observed: "It is through fantasy that children achieve catharsis. It is the best means they have for taming the Wild Things."

Bruno Bettelheim advances similar arguments in his award-winning *The Uses of Enchantment*, where he defends fairy tales from experts and censors who argue that the young shouldn't be exposed to hair-raising stories about the wolf who devours Little Red Riding Hood, the witch who would kill Snow White, and the stepmother who mistreats Cinderella. In response, Bettelheim offers three arguments in favor of the fairy tales' presentation of scary incidents and characters: (1) instead of deceiving children, the tales frankly and honestly acknowledge that evil exists in the world; (2) instead of belittling or ignoring children's fears by sweeping them under the rug, fairy tales directly present and address them; and (3) these old stories present models and lessons suggesting that (with pluck and courage and cleverness) children, themselves, can become heroes and heroines who can master evildoers and their own fears. Making the case for scary stories and putting the argument for mastery in a nutshell, Bettelheim asks: If there is no witch to push in the oven, how can Hansel and Gretel become heroes?

Discomforting Fun

Kids enjoy being scared. You will find more youngsters than adults on roller coasters. They tell frightening stories at slumber parties. Halloween is great fun. And of all God's creatures, the favorite of the very young is the dinosaur—an animal that has the great advantage of being both horrific and extinct. There is something paradoxical in these delights because the fundamental feeling of being frightened is acute discomfort.

Consider the physical symptoms of fear. It is a *visceral* experience: our flesh creeps, we get goosebumps, we break out in a cold sweat. We turn "white as a sheet" or "pale as a ghost." Like the moment in MGM's *The Wizard of Oz* when Dorothy and her companions begin to worry ("Lions and Tigers and Bears, Oh My!"), we rattle like the Tinman: we tremble, we shake and shudder, we shiver and quiver. When we are scared, we feel like Ichabod Crane in "The Legend of Sleepy Hollow" in his encounter with the Headless Horseman: "his teeth chattered," "his heart began to thump," his hair "rose on his head," and "his parched tongue clove to the roof of his mouth."

Besides these physical symptoms, the state of fear also creates emotional distress. When we are afraid, instead of calm or indifference or delight, we feel anxious, terrified, stricken, alarmed, and threatened. We have misgivings, qualms, apprehensions. We hesitate, wince, shrink, cower, shy, flinch. A sense of danger and panic, of peril and dread, plays havoc with us.

Mentally, we are also a wreck. On the one hand, when we are frightened, the mind shuts down: we are "scared out of our wits" and lose our equanimity. On the other hand, in heightened states of fear, the mind becomes intensely alert, on the lookout for threats, in an exhausting state of tension and anticipation.

Given these considerable and acute forms of distress, how can children enjoy being scared? Or, for that matter, how can youngsters find fun in reading or hearing terrifying tales?

To answer those questions, we need to consider what happens when we play the game of "Boo" with infants or say "Grrr" while

Mercer Mayer, *There's a Nightmare in My Closet* (Dial, 1968).
© 1968 by Mercer Mayer.

pretending to be a pursuing monster. At first, the baby is startled: blood rushes from the face, eyes open wide, the mouth forms into an O, and the child holds its breath. It is as if the organism shrinks away from possible pain. But in the next moment, the tide turns; the baby is amused at our antics, laughs, blood comes rushing back to the face, and eyes twinkle. In the pleasurable experience of scariness, shock is followed by delight.

But consider another occasion when the game of "Boo" does not go well—when, for example, a stranger says "Boo" to the infant, and the baby is genuinely startled and ends up crying and shivering, retreating and seeking solace from a parent. What is the difference between these two situations?

When the baby is delighted, scariness takes place in a context, a history (as it were) that the child has learned. This is a "game," the child recognizes, "like other times we have played." This is familiar. This is a "pretend threat, and I am in no real danger." When the game of "Boo" does not go well, however, these conditions and contexts are absent, and there is no security net. In one case, after the fright, blood does not return to the baby's face; the child remains blanched and shivering, and the return to vividness seems arrested at a point where the threat remains paramount. In the other case, blood returns to the baby's face and, in pleasure, the infant seems more vividly alive. In one situation the self seems endangered and diminished, while in the other we see a more vivid self in response.

Whether threatening or pleasurable, scariness confirms the experience of *living*. The shock comes from "outside." It threatens *us*. It wakes us up. In moments of reverie or self-absorption, shock is a sudden reminder that a world exists apart from us and might do us harm; shock wakes up even the most dreamy solipsist. Moreover, it vividly wakes "us" up. It prompts reaction from the "inside," a concern for "self" preservation.

Here, then, lies an explanation of why the discomfort of scariness may be fun and why the young paradoxically find pleasure when their teeth chatter, their hearts thump, and their hair stands on end. Being frightened is stimulating and thrilling because it wakes up a more vivid self in response. Likewise, contextualized in something like the safety net of the game of "Boo," the proximate encounter with pain in the fiction of a scary story evokes a more intense feeling of being alive and heightened recognition of being an individual.

This relation between fiction and safety is important to understand. There are child-raising experts who insist that the young should be exposed only to harmless stories free of scary characters and incidents, to saccharine and expurgated tales where happy teddy bears always picnic in the forest. These high-minded censors base their argument on the contention that the young are unable to distinguish between fact and fiction and, as a result, will be genuinely terrified. This old saw needs to be put to rest. And we can do so by asking a question: At what age do children recognize the difference between fact and fiction? The answer to that is another question: At what age does the baby laugh when we play the game of "Boo"?

When scary stories are understood as a kind of game and fiction, the simulated encounter with the threatening is one of childhood's great pleasures because of the thrilling vividness of individuality it wakes up in response. Shivering in anxiety when a witch threatens Dorothy in *The Wizard of Oz*, getting goosebumps when Max encounters monsters in *Where the Wild Things Are*, trembling when Little Red Riding Hood meets the wolf, the young understand that children's stories can be discomforting fun.

3
SMALLNESS

More than adults, children are fascinated with the issue of size and particularly with smallness. Only in Children's Literature is littleness so frequent a topic (Snow White's companions, the size of Cinderella's shoe, Alice's shrinking, Dorothy among the Munchkins, etc.), and only in that genre does the word *little* appear so frequently in titles ("Little Red Riding Hood," *Little Women*, *The Little Prince*, *A Little Princess*, *The Little Engine That Could*, *Little Lord Fauntleroy*, *Little House on the Prairie*, etc.). With the exception of a few adult books (Günter Grass's *Tin Drum*, for example, and Art Spiegelman's *Maus*), juveniles seem to own the terrain of the miniature: where mouselike Stuart Little drives a wind-up car, the hedgehog Miss Tiggy-Winkle washes the tiny clothes of animals, and there is an Indian in the

Beatrix Potter, *The Tailor of Gloucester*
(Warne, 1903).

cupboard as well as a cricket in Times Square. And with the exception of the cult classic *Fantastic Voyage* (where Raquel Welch and a medical team are shrunk and inserted into a human body), children's films also seem to have a monopoly on the minuscule: *Antz, A Bug's Life, The Rescuers, The Secret of NIMH, Toy Story, Finding Nemo,* and others.

Of course, the fascination of the young with smallness may be explained in terms of their size, but it is also a reflection of their diminished power. As for dwarves and midgets (with whom children are often compared), littleness is a handicap in a larger-scaled world where restaurants obligingly provide high chairs and booster seats along with wheelchair access. Even if the mini-young can see over the countertops at McDonald's, tots are powerless in other ways and can't, for example, pay for their order with a credit card. This conflation of size and power, Erik Erickson suggests in *Childhood and Society,* gets internalized as we grow up: "Every adult was once a child. He was once small. A sense of smallness forms a substratum in his mind, ineradicably. His triumphs will be measured against his smallness; his defeats will substantiate it. The questions as to who is bigger and who can do this or that, and to whom—these questions fill the adult's inner life." In a film fantasy, Tom Hanks is magically transformed from a boy into an adult with a Manhattan apartment and a position as a Madison Avenue executive: the movie is called *Big*. Also linking power and size, billionaire Leona Helmsley famously said, "Only the little people pay taxes."

In terms of altitude, children constitute an overlooked underclass. Adults wink over the tops of their heads; in that sense, they resemble Ralph Ellison's Invisible Man. Marginalized mites in an outsized world of towering adults—that race of creatures Kenneth Grahame called "the Olympians"—our Tom Thumbs and Thumbelinas might well view the movie title *Honey, I Shrunk the Kids* as a gratuitous cultural admission.

Of course, in the subversive manner of the dispossessed, small fry can also turn a disadvantage into an advantage. This is reflected in their reading. Peter Rabbit eludes Mr. McGregor by popping through a window where his portly pursuer cannot follow. Stuart Little, while dwarfed by New York City, is puny enough to slip down a sink drain and retrieve a lost wedding ring. The miniature rascals in Potter's *The Tale of Two Bad Mice* are able to furnish their home with purloined possessions from a dollhouse. And like the conventional circus dwarf who routinely outwits the giant, Jack (once he ascends the beanstalk) and Perrault's Tom Thumb (*Petit Poucet*) have their ways with humongous ogres and their wives.

E. B. White, *Stuart Little* (Harper & Brothers, 1945). Illustration
by Garth Williams. © 1945, renewed 1973 by Garth Williams.

Better even than diminutive heroes, however, are miniature worlds where the young can enjoy adult perquisites and tower godlike over creation. Children spend hours moving tiny figurines about on the rug. Equally suggestive, "the heart of Legoland"—says the Web site for this California theme park intended for kids between the ages of two and twelve—is Miniland: a "celebration of American achievements" on a scale of 1 to 20, where the young (say, in relation to a replica of the Statue of Liberty) are about as proportionate as King Kong to the Empire State Building.

Microcosms

Musing on the topic of scale, Robert Louis Stevenson wrote that everyone who recalls childhood "must remember laying his head in the grass, staring into the infinitesimal forest and seeing it grow populous with fairy armies." The busy worlds of ants and worms and other insects seem to invite in the young a notion of minute and populous universes, concurrent realms where might exist a race of tiny humans. Indeed, when Lemuel Gulliver falls asleep on such a grassy sward in Lilliput, he is soon trussed up by an army of six-inch-high soldiers.

While not originally meant for children but later adopted by them, Jonathan Swift's *Gulliver's Travels* shows the special pleasure in tracing out the implications of a premise. If the hero is twelve times larger than the Lilliputians, Gulliver must crawl on hands and knees through the gate of the castle, his meals consist of barrels of wine and vats of meat, children play in his hair, horses and sheep are only a few inches high, and when Gulliver urinates or defecates it is something of an environmental disaster. In this sense, the Tiny Tale is a microcosmic game: so Hans Andersen's Thumbelina sleeps in a walnut shell and is "pelted" by snowflakes, and E. B. White's mouse-sized Stuart Little is reasonably afraid of cats and must manage the logistics of a straw when a shopkeeper provides him with a glass of sarsaparilla. At the opposite end of the scale, this is equally true in the Tall Tale: when, for example, Gulliver travels on to the giants' domain of Brobdingnag, he must climb six-foot-high stairs; and when Paul Bunyan wants pancakes, he requires a griddle the size of a lake and employs lumberjacks to skate across it with bacon tied to their feet in order to grease the pan.

Among miniaturists, an author to reckon with is Beatrix Potter—a woman who accepted her first marriage proposal when her suitor presented her with a dollhouse, an accomplished amateur mycologist who produced incredibly detailed drawings of fungi by staring into a microscope, and a secretive person who kept a diary in such tiny handwriting that it was decades before someone had the patience to decode it. Among her little books, her favorite was *The Tailor of Gloucester*, which tells of a complete and parallel mouse world behind the walls of the town's old houses. With their own staircases and trapdoors, their own society and occupations, their own clothes and customs, these mice carry on with little notice from humans and in an alternate cosmos of encyclopedic completeness, at once epic and domestic.

This story of seamstress mice—Margaret Lane has suggested in her biography *The Tale of Beatrix Potter*—was inspired by Potter's radical cousin Caroline, who was concerned with the underpaid and underappreciated women who sewed embroidered dresses and labored like medieval miniaturists on every jot and tittle of these garments. But the existence of a complete and separate world behind the walls and within our own world might also be said to reflect the situation of children within the world of adults: when the nursery is a room apart from others in the house, when children are to be "seen but not heard" or (as with the case of mice) "heard but not seen"—a separate-but-equal apartheid between young and old rephrased as a segregation between animals and humans.

Although humans never cross the threshold and inhabit nutshell worlds in Potter's tales, in Mary Norton's *The Borrowers* a race of six-inch-high and entirely human people live under the floorboards of an old country home in England. This is the story of the Clock family—the enterprising Pod, his squeamish spouse Homily, and their daughter Arrietty—who are among the last of a dying race of Borrowers who prosper on the leavings of the giant "human beans" who live upstairs. In their sequestered little nest, the Clocks decorate with framed postage stamps, statuary of chess pieces, and rugs composed of blotting paper. To get by, Pod must occasionally leave the security of home to scavenge: dangerously scaling a curtain by means of a safety pin and thread, for example, to "borrow" something from a high shelf. More often, the Clocks are huddled at home because the great danger is "being seen," since that would mean the arrival of the ratcatcher, as happens in the conclusion when the Clocks are forced into exile.

Among readers, it has been something of a parlor game to suggest whom the Borrowers represent. Norton's own remarks seem to imply she had in mind the poor during the economic hard times of the 1930s: an invisible and separate race, as it were, that lived on others' scraps. Then, too, Norton lived through World War II, and her subsequent book (1952) may picture the British sheltering during the Blitz; in the fear of "being seen," it may resemble *The Diary of Anne Frank*. On my part, I would add two other possibilities. The first is the Travelers, the Tinkers of

Mary Norton, *The Borrowers* (Harcourt, Brace & World, 1953).
Illustration by Diana Stanley. © 1953, 1952 by Mary Norton and
renewed 1981, 1980 by Mary Norton, Beth Krush, and Joe Krush.

Ireland and the British Isles, a race apart with a reputation for "borrowing." The other possibility is the Irish themselves, a nationality especially known for its stories about "the little people" and, until recently, often employed as downstairs help in the Big Houses.

Norton's diminutions are also related to gender. Arrietty is kept behind locked passageways and indoors by her frightened parents. Nonetheless, very much in the spirit of Jo March in Louisa May Alcott's pointedly named *Little Women*, Arrietty is a Little Girl who hazards forays into the outside world without parental permission and discovers a wonderfully larger realm, where she encounters the Boy, as well as a world of sunshine. Learning of these dangerous escapades, but only because they have no son, her parents reluctantly agree that Arrietty shall be allowed to follow in her father's footsteps and be tutored in the ways of borrowing. In many respects, Norton's novel is the story of Arrietty and the Little Girl's liberation.

But *The Borrowers* may also be said especially to picture the situation of the young, and this explains the appeal of the book to children. Late in his life, the Boy (one of the few full-sized humans who comes in contact with this tiny race and treats them sympathetically) speculates about the origins of the Borrowers: "Underneath, he thought they were frightened.

It was because they were frightened, he thought, that they had grown so small. Each generation had become smaller and smaller, and more hidden and more hidden." The powerlessness of the young and the vulnerability of the small explain the aroma of timidity and agoraphobia that hovers over Norton's presentation of this tiny world. The marginalized Borrowers are essentially voyeurs in a realm of giants, echoing the situation of children in the company of adults.

As we observed when discussing Snugness, this existential feeling of being dwarfed in the universe is common among children. We mentioned how Laura Ingalls Wilder, when describing her own childhood experiences in *The Little House on the Prairie*, said: "All around them there was nothing but grassy prairie spreading to the edge of the sky. . . . The land and the sky seemed too large, and Laura felt small." This sentiment is acute in *The Borrowers*, with its frequent visions of the anxious Clocks huddled in their home, worried about jeopardy if they move in the Larger World.

Focal Range

Looking back at his childhood in *Grace before Ploughing*, John Masefield recalled something that others may remember from their own childhoods: how he paid attention to things close at hand and could stare for hours into his box of toys and marbles. Focal range, the kind of thing optometrists measure, varies as we get older: at first, the very young are almost myopic and intimately know their room and home; growing older, children's boundaries of attention widen to include their neighborhood and school; and in adulthood, horizons widen to even larger geographic spans. In fact, it may be that a certain focal range (just where our gaze should fall and how wide attention should be) is something we are socialized into accepting; driving a car in traffic, for example, requires adults to share a certain visual consensus and forfeit other focal ranges. In any event, there is an observable difference between the way the young and the old *see* life; as Masefield says, "The child knows his mile, or at most his two miles, better than a grown-up knows his parish."

For Mary Norton, these ocular observations had a quite literal side. She was nearsighted as a child, and this wasn't diagnosed until she was sent off to boarding school; soon after, she was provided with glasses. In a letter to an acquaintance, she tells how the memory of her childhood without corrective lenses prompted the writing of *The Borrowers*. Referring to herself in the third person, Norton recalls the implications of her impaired vision:

For her brothers, walks with her must have been something of a trial: she was an inveterate lingerer, a gazer into banks and hedgerows, a rapt investigator of shallow pools, a lier-down by stream-like teeming ditches. Such walks were punctuated by [her brothers'] loud, long-suffering cries: "Oh, come on . . . for goodness' sake . . . What on earth are you staring at now? . . . Look, there's a buzzard! There! On the post!" But it wasn't like a buzzard to her: there was a post (or something like a post) slightly thickened at the top. "There she goes! What a beauty!" The thickened end of the post had broken off and she saw for a second a swift, dim shadow of flight, and the post seemed a great deal shorter.

For this nearsighted child, then, it was easy to imagine a race of wee people living close at hand and among the ants: "She saw through their eyes the great lava-like (sometimes almost steaming) lakes of cattle dung, the pock-like craters in the mud—chasms to them, whether wet or dry. It would take them, she thought, almost half an hour of tottering on ridges, helping one another, calling out warnings, holding one another's hands before, exhausted, they reached the dry grass beyond."

Then the miraculous spectacles arrived at school, and Mary Norton saw like the rest of us. The homunculi were forgotten, only to be recalled later.

Growing Up and Looking Down

There is a curious moment in *The Borrowers* when Arrietty has been granted tentative admission into maturity and, as an apprentice borrower, sees her father in the distance. Always living in close proximity to her family, Arrietty is startled when she accompanies Pod on her first foraging expedition and sees him scuttle away and across an upstairs hallway: "Suddenly she saw him as '*small.*'" Besides her apprehension of a surprising correlation between distance and smallness, Arrietty's entrance into maturity can also be understood as a demythologizing of her father and a diminishing of the grandeur he possessed in her childhood. Indeed, it is striking how often growing *up* in Children's Literature means looking *down* and be-littling.

A similar story is told in Andersen's "The Snow Queen," when the boy Kay begins to see things differently. Before, he was a child devoted to picture stories of the Infant Jesus, his grandmother, and his companion, Gerda. Then he "looks down." After looking at a snowflake under a microscope, he changes into a jeering adolescent who belittles the things of childhood, calling picture books "baby stuff," mimicking his grandmother, and teasing Gerda.

Looking down also plays a part in Heidi's growing up. When she first arrives on her mountaintop, the youngster asks about the hawk that always circles above and cries and screams. Her misanthropic grandfather tells her the bird is jeering: "He is mocking the people who live down below in the villages, because they all go huddling and gossiping together, and encourage one another in evil talking and deeds." Later in the book, during her crucial experiences in Frankfurt, an older Heidi deliberately seeks out a high bell tower where she can look down on the city; then she observes, "If the hawk were to fly over Frankfurt, he would complain even louder about people huddling all together and teaching each other evil ways, rather than going to live in the mountains, where it is so much better."

From Heidi's bell tower, from the ramparts of heaven, *sub specie aeternitatis*, in the distances of space, how "little" (in the sense of "petty" or "insignificant") seem human endeavors. How shortsighted. How small-minded.

In the company of the giants of Brobdingnag, a minuscule Gulliver tells the king about his life and the culture of England. Listening to his tiny companion describe the ways of his similar-sized and antlike countrymen, the giant monarch sighs about the vanity of the world: "How contemptible a thing was human grandeur, which could be mimicked by such diminutive insects

Charles Perrault, "Le Petit poucet" ["Little Tom Thumb"],
in *Les Contes de Perrault* (Hetzel, 1867). Illustration by Gustave Doré.

Diego Rodriguez Velázquez, *Las Meninas*, 1656.
Oil on canvas. Museo del Prado, Madrid.

as I: and yet, said he, I dare engage, these creatures have their titles and distinctions of honour, they contrive little nests and burrows, that they call houses and cities; they love, they fight, they dispute, they cheat, they betray."

Importance

So much depends upon a sense of scale. When Arrietty sees her father in the distance, she is impressed by how small this adult and his pastimes seem. From the point of view of adults, on the other hand, children (tots, small fry, urchins, moppets, tykes, ragamuffins, bambinos, cherubs, and waifs) are often "cute"—endearing but small and thereby insignificant. The young and old disagree on each others' notions of importance.

Take Velázquez's famous painting *Las Meninas*. The center of interest is the five-year-old Infanta, Doña Margarita, who doesn't want to pose for the portrait. Others surrounding her—the bending and beckoning maids (the Meninas), even her parents (miniaturized by their reflection in the distant mirror)—are attentive to this youngster and trying to placate her. Velázquez criticizes this child-centeredness, this paying of too much attention to a child. This is indicated by his self-portrait: his appearance as the painter in the picture, who exchanges with the viewer a bemused and long-suffering look, as if to say, "Can you believe this? The way they take this child's tantrum seriously? This tempest in a teapot?"

But Velázquez's criticism of misplaced importance is indicated even more by issues of size and the painting's proportions: all this busy child-centeredness occupies, as it were, the bottom fifth of the painting and is disproportionate to the other four-fifths of the room and the painting. In the greater sense of things, Velázquez seems to be saying, all the attention paid this doted-upon and foregrounded five-year-old is incommensurate and out of scale: children *are* small, *ergo* insignificant. Equally revealing is the inclusion, on the right, of Maribarbola, the child's female dwarf; the dwarf is, as Kenneth Clark suggests, "a disturbing element" by which Velázquez presents again a sense of disproportion, a "stunted" adult, and something out of scale.

Contrast this painting with John Singer Sargent's famous portrait *The Daughters of Edward D. Boit*. There seems nothing unusual about the foregrounded child sitting on the rug, nor the girl to the left, with hands clasped behind her. But as the eye drifts farther back, we see two older girls standing in the shadows and dwarfed by a huge porcelain vase; another massive china jar stands nearby. It is an Alice in Wonderland–like

John Singer Sargent, *The Daughters of Edward Darley Boit*, 1882.
Oil on canvas. © Museum of Fine Arts, Boston.

moment, and our sense of scale is suddenly jarred. It is as if we suddenly realize we are in Miniland, and this prompts a revision of our original notion of how close we must be in viewing this world of theirs.

So much depends upon a sense of scale. The shift in proportions from Velázquez's *Las Meninas* to Sargent's child-centered painting resembles a moment in *Gulliver's Travels* when the tiny Lilliputians file a report on the contents of Gulliver's pockets and describe in detail a prodigiously long wooden pillar, in the middle of which is a steel plate besmirched with a white substance. Under the microscope, as it were, such an ordinary thing as a razor suddenly seems wondrous. With a shift of scale, from the point of view of Sargent's children, the small opens up to a vastness.

So much depends upon a sense of scale. For adults, as television news suggests, events in the Larger World are important. In the smaller world of the child, however, the blooming of the tomato plant outside the window may be more significant than any election, but it never gets reported by television broadcasters. With different senses of scale, the old and young disagree on issues of importance. E. B. White's mouselike character Stuart Little, for example, is able to identify with children because of his size. On the day he serves as a substitute teacher, he and the youngsters come to agreement about what's really important in life: "A shaft of sunlight at the end of a dark afternoon, a note of music, and the way the back of a baby's neck smells if its mother keeps it tidy."

The small worlds of Children's Literature, in other words, present alternatives to consensual notions of dimension and, consequently, adult notions of importance. That is no small thing. Indeed, encountering a Miniland in Children's Literature, we might repeat Jan Morris's admiring comment about the country of Wales: "Its smallness is not petty; on the contrary, it is profound."

P. L. Travers, *Mary Poppins* (Reynal & Hitchcock, 1934).
Illustration by Mary Shepard, hand-tinted by
Denise DeLuise. © 1934, renewed 1962 by P. L. Travers.

LIGHTNESS

In Steven Spielberg's movie *Hook*, his imagined sequel to J. M. Barrie's *Peter Pan*, Peter has grown up and forgotten who he was. Instead of a lighthearted sprite, Peter has become our contemporary: a forty-year-old workaholic weighed down by responsibilities and tied to his cell phone. Over the course of the film, Spielberg's Peter must eventually remember his childhood and recover his lightness so he can fly again.

The clash between lightness and heaviness is a conspicuous theme in Children's Literature. This may not be surprising, since childhood is a time when the young are dazzled by kites and helium-filled balloons, when they zoom on skateboards or don capes that permit them to soar like Superman. As a result, in Children's Literature (with its world of flying carpets, winged fairies, aerial heroes, and witches on broomsticks), characters are more likely to go airborne than in adult fare.

In Hans Christian Andersen's fairy tales, for example, issues of lightness and weight predominate. A moment in "The Ugly Duckling" is representative. At one point, the Duckling is swimming in a lake, sees a flock of swans flying overhead, and feels strongly drawn to those unreachable, airborne creatures. But that image is immediately followed by another as the Duckling is locked into the ice when the lake freezes over.

In Andersen's tales, visions of fixity and flight alternate. Throughout much of her story, Thumbelina seems an invalid, and her immobility is not remedied until the end when this fairy finally gets her wings. In "The Girl Who Trod on a Loaf," Inger is transformed into a statue in hell and remains that way for years, until a child's prayers rescue her and she becomes a bird that flies up to heaven. And even when she gets her new set of legs, the Little Mermaid is constricted in another way, since she becomes mute and is unable to communicate with her beloved prince; in the conclusion, she is finally released from gravity and joins the spirits of the air.

The process of petrification that overcomes so many of Andersen's characters can be understood by turning to William Steig's remarkably direct picture book *Sylvester and the Magic*

Pebble. Young Sylvester finds a pebble that grants all his wishes. When he encounters a lion, however, he is (quite literally) petrified with fear; using his magic pebble, hastily wishing he was a rock, he is changed into just that. Frozen in stone, suffering the fate of Lot's wife, Sylvester is lost and lonely; he cannot communicate with others, and his parents are unable (until the very end) to find and rescue him.

In an interview with Jonathan Cott, Steig made clear how his ideas for *Sylvester* were inspired by his work with Wilhelm Reich, the psychotherapist. Reich was interested in how emotional experiences are translated into muscular events: how, over time, individuals become rigid and stiff, sclerotic and blocked, in response to feeling thwarted or obstructed; how maturation involves the construction of "body armor" as a defense mechanism to perceived threats; and how this muscular rigidity is accompanied by feelings of being unloved, helpless, and unable to communicate. The applicability of Reich's ideas to *Sylvester* may be immediately apparent, and it takes only a little more consideration to see their applicability to Andersen's stories about the unloved Duckling, invalid Thumbelina, and mute Mermaid.

The opposite of the person with body armor, Reich proposed, is the person who can give into "flow": childlike individuals who are fluid and mobile and light. Advocating this, Reich was sympathetically disposed to dance, to massage (as a way of relaxing muscles once tensed in fear and now habitually cramped), and to orgasmic experiences of surrender. Ultimately, Reich's paragon is someone who doesn't respond to life with fear and anxiety but remains flexible and free.

The great symbol for Reich's fluid and light personality might well be J. M. Barrie's Peter Pan—that nimble and agile *Puer Aeternus*, airborne with fairy dust and happy thoughts and accompanied by that shooting star Tinkerbell. "I'm youth, I'm joy," he tells his antagonist Captain Hook. And he is that. But he is also Puck and a lighthearted mischief-maker in a dynamic world where the chase is everything.

In one sense, there are two forces at work in Barrie's *Peter Pan*. One is represented by Tinkerbell, a kind of hyperbolic version of Peter's youthful and aerial mobility. Unlike Andersen's invalid Thumbelina, this fairy is a vector of light and dynamic energy, minute and mercurial, plastic and evanescent. She resembles Lucretius's vision of the atom, a tiny bit of matter streaking through space and given to unpredictable swerves, or she resembles our technologies' bits of information zooming around and crackling in the world we inhabit.

Opposite this image of extraordinary mobility is Captain Hook. While Tinkerbell is fluid and mercurial, Hook is an

"Peter Soared Out into the Night," in *Peter Pan's A B C*
(Hodder & Stoughton, n.d. [ca. 1914]). Illustration by Flora White.

adult with an imposing and fixed presence, evil incarnate and a grand seigneur dressed in the finery associated with Charles II and the Stuart era. And while Tinkerbell is a force of swerves of freedom and whimsicality, Hook insists on and is preoccupied with "Good Form" and "Bad Form." And unlike the unfettered fairy, Hook is hobbled.

On several occasions, in moments of intertextual play, Barrie compares his pirate villain to the limping Long John Silver (the buccaneer and rogue in *Treasure Island*, created by Barrie's friend and fellow Scotsman, Robert Louis Stevenson). But while Silver limps around on his peg leg, Hook's name reminds us that he has lost another body part to a crocodile—or, more particularly, to a croc who has swallowed a clock, a time bomb (of sorts) that eventually gets him. In fact, in Barrie's novel, the ticking clock is the real enemy and a symbol of how maturity is always stealing up on us.

Because that's how it is in Barrie's novel: youth is a perishable thing. The tragic moment in Barrie's *Peter Pan* occurs at the end when Peter, after an absence of some years, revisits Wendy. When she steps into the light, Peter gives a sharp cry of pain and asks, "What is it?" Wendy replies, "I am old." And indeed, moments earlier, the now aged Wendy had explained to her daughter why she can no longer fly: "I am grown up, dearest.... It is only the gay and innocent and heartless who can fly."

In Barrie's *Peter Pan*, aerial mobility is the perquisite of the young, and the loss of lightness is the inevitable price of maturity. In his sequel *Hook*, however, Spielberg offers what might be called the crocodile codicil: that needn't be the case for the adult who can remember and recover his or her childhood.

Varieties of Lightness

There may be no better example of the impulse toward lightness than the opening of Kenneth Grahame's *The Wind in the Willows*, when Mole abandons his subterranean home:

The Mole had been working very hard all the morning, spring-cleaning his little home. First with brooms, then with dusters; then on ladders and steps and chairs, with a brush and a pail of whitewash; till he had dust in his throat and eyes, and splashes of whitewash all over his black fur, and an aching back and weary arms. Spring was moving in the air above and in the earth below and around him, penetrating even his dark and lowly little house with its spirit of divine discontent and longing. It was small wonder, then, that he suddenly flung down his brush on the floor, said "Bother!" and "O blow!" and also "Hang spring-cleaning!" and bolted out of the house without even waiting to put on his coat. Something up above was calling him imperiously, and he made for [his] steep little tunnel.... So he scraped and scratched and scrabbled and scrooged and then he scrooged again and scrabbled and scratched and scraped, working busily with his little paws and muttering to himself, "Up we go! Up we go!" till at last, pop! his snout came out into the sunlight, and he found himself rolling in the warm grass of a great meadow. "This is fine!" he said to himself. "This is better than whitewashing!"

This upward vision of liberation opens the book, and Grahame ends that chapter by observing that this was the first of many similar days for the "emancipated" Mole. Indeed, in the pages that follow, Mole embarks on a Vita Nuova, a new life full of adventure.

But, as we have intimated in our discussions of Snugness and Scariness, there is another impulse also at work in *The Wind in the Willows*. The vision of Mole's liberation from his home, his movement upward from his subterranean enclosure, is balanced by several other moments in the story where pleasure comes in the opposite way: by a descent into snug abodes. Lost in the Wild Woods and afraid in the midst of a snowstorm, Mole is greatly relieved when he and Ratty find Badger's cozy, subterranean home and take refuge there. Leaving later, during an arduous journey through the snow, Mole scents his own, old home, and he and Ratty descend and take comfort there. Then Mole feels the opposite pleasure of homecoming and the familiar.

In a sense, the dynamic dialectic present within Mole is embodied in two separate characters in the novel. That great rascal Toad is a force of lightness who is often seen outside his home and on the move (streaking by in his rowing scull, embarking on a jaunt in his gypsy cart, roaring over the countryside in his motorcar); he constantly seeks the new and is given to fads. Opposite him is Badger, an image of weight: a stationary and stay-at-home adult who is solid and fixed and settled. And if Toad is given to fads, Badger may be remembered by the moment when he takes Mole to see some Roman ruins and observes that, while people come and go, "we [badgers] remain." Toad is careless and cheeky, impulsive and mercurial, while Badger is responsible and peremptory, grave and stolid. And while Toad is a mischievous rascal and a rule breaker, Badger functions as warden and policeman, a guardian and an adult who puts the rowdy Toad in his place. If Toad is lighthearted youth, Badger is maturity and gravity. If Toad is a highflier, Badger is his kryptonite.

With these understandings in place, we can begin to sharpen our understanding of lightness. First and simply, we might note that lightness and weight are often paired, and lightness stands out by contrast. But the example of Badger also prompts another observation: the quality of weight can be commendable,

"The Origin of Superman," in *Amazing World of Superman*,
Metropolis Edition (National Periodical Publications, 1973).
Illustration by Carmine Infantino, Curt Swan, Murphy
Anderson, and E. Nelson Bridwell. © 1973 by DC Comics.

too. Though Badger is a gruff adult, he is kindly and likable as well. In discussing lightness, then, my suggestion is not that weight doesn't have its own virtues. Instead, in emphasizing lightness, I am suggesting that this quality is more conspicuous among children and has a more important role in Children's Literature. To say this differently, while many children may wish to be the rascally Toad and some may identify with the curious Mole, in my experience no child has ever wished to be Badger.

We can also more closely describe the quality of lightness by examining the opening of another book, Mark Twain's *The Adventures of Tom Sawyer*. In this scene, Aunt Polly catches her mischievous nephew in the pantry, filching jam:

There was a slight noise behind her and she turned just in time to seize a small boy by the slack of his roundabout and arrest his flight. "There! I might 'a' thought of that closet. What you been doing in there?"

"Nothing."

"Nothing! Look at your hands. And look at your mouth. What is that truck?"

"I don't know, aunt."

"Well, I know. It's jam—that's what it is. Forty times I've said if you didn't let that jam alone I'd skin you. Hand me that switch."

The switch hovered in the air—the peril was desperate—

"My! Look behind you, aunt!"

The old lady whirled round, and snatched her skirts out of danger. The lad fled on the instant, scrambled up the high board-fence, and disappeared over it. His Aunt Polly stood surprised a moment, and then broke into a gentle laugh.

This scene might serve as an emblem for the entire book, and the first thing to notice is Tom's nimbleness as he leaps over the fence. Agile, Tom is quick on his feet, sneaking out of the house or playing hooky, escaping the tedium of church and the boredom of school, eluding Aunt Polly and evading Injun Joe. Lightness, in other words, is not just a quality of airborne characters like Peter Pan. It also includes the spry, the lithe, and the quick.

But another part of that scene is also associated with lightness, and that is evident in the trick Tom plays on Aunt Polly, getting her to look around so he can make his escape. Cleverness is the mobility of intelligence, and Tom Sawyer has this in aces. Most memorable, of course, is the scene where Tom persuades his friends to whitewash the fence. With mental legerdemain, Tom converts a chore into a glamorous opportunity afforded to only a few, and soon there is a long line of hoodwinked boys paying Tom for the privilege of painting the fence. Tom entices his companion with his question, "Does a boy get a chance to whitewash a fence every day?" and, as Clemens observes, "That put things in a new light." And this is Tom's genius, seen often in the book: his ability to shift perspectives, his facile wit, a lightness not only of his feet but also of his mind.

The final thing to note about the jam-stealing scene is Aunt Polly's reaction when she is outfoxed by Tom: she "stood surprised a moment, then broke into a gentle laugh." Tom is a mischievous scamp, a picaro, an endearing rascal. So, too, is Toad in *The Wind in the Willows*. So, too, is Peter Rabbit, whom the sympathetic Beatrix Potter describes as "naughty." And among mischief-makers, there is also that imp Peter Pan. They are all cousins of Puck and, like Aunt Polly, our spirits are lifted and we take subversive delight in their lightsome ways as they upset rules and evade the authorities. Mischief, we observe, is another form of lightness.

But there is still one more way Twain's novel can be useful in a description of lightness, and that lies in Clemens's handling of melodrama. In one scene, Aunt Polly gives Tom a swat in the mistaken belief that he has broken a sugar bowl, when the damage was actually done by another. Tom is aggrieved at this injustice, and Clemens humorously describes Tom's self-indulgent sorrow:

Tom sulked in a corner and exalted his woes. He knew that in her heart his aunt was on her knees to him, and he was morosely gratified by the consciousness of it. He would hang out no signals, he would take notice of none. He knew that a yearning glance fell upon him, now and then, through a film of tears, but he refused recognition of it. He pictured himself lying sick unto death and his aunt bending over him beseeching one little forgiving word, but he would turn his face to the wall, and die with that word unsaid. Ah, how would she feel then? And he pictured himself brought home from the river, dead, with his curls all wet, and his sore heart at rest. How she would throw herself upon him, and how her tears would fall like rain, and her lips pray God to give her back her boy and she would never, never abuse him any more! But he would lie there cold and white and make no sign—a poor little sufferer, whose griefs were at an end. He so worked upon his feelings with the pathos of these dreams, that he had to keep swallowing, he was so like to choke; and his eyes swam in a blur of water, which overflowed when he winked, and ran down and trickled from the end of his nose. And such a luxury to him was this petting of his sorrows, that he could not bear to have any worldly cheeriness or any grating delight intrude upon it; it was too sacred for such contact; and so, presently, when his cousin Mary danced in, all alive with the joy of seeing home again after an age-long visit of one week to the country, he got up and moved in clouds and darkness out at one door as she brought song and sunshine in at the other.

Melodrama is tragedy from which weight has been subtracted, and there are other similar scenes in the novel that are equally amusing—when, for example, Tom doesn't want to go to school and lies in his deathbed suffering from a terminal toothache, or when Becky Thatcher jilts Tom and the heartbroken boy decides to run away and (in effect) join the French Foreign Legion. Such scenes are, of course, a burlesque of adults and their romantic fiction, with its indulgent melancholia and extravagant heartaches; in this way, Twain's novel is a sort of hilarious and juvenile parody of, say, the *Sturm und Drang* of Goethe's *The Sorrows of Young Werther*. To say this differently: by means of melodrama, Clemens "makes light" of Tom's troubles and cares.

But there is one final way we might refine our understanding of lightness. In *Six Memos for the Next Millennium*, Italo Calvino wrote, "Lightness for me goes with precision and determination, not with vagueness and the haphazard." By way of illustration, he quotes Paul Valéry: "One should be light like a bird, not like a feather."

This kind of lighthearted precision appears in a serious moment near the end of Robert Louis Stevenson's *Treasure Island*. With dagger in hand, the injured pirate Israel Hands begins to stalk Jim Hawkins and attempts to box the boy into a corner on the deck of the *Hispaniola*. But Jim doesn't accept the seriousness of the situation. He responds with lightness. For him, "it was a boy's game," a game of hide-and-seek. And eventually, the spry boy outmaneuvers and overcomes the slow-moving adult.

Throughout Stevenson's book, Jim is clever and nimble and agile—as clever as Toad escaping a pursuing posse of policemen, as nimble as Tom Sawyer leaping over Aunt Polly's fence, as agile as Peter Rabbit slipping under Mr. McGregor's fence. Jim is saved by his dancing gait, his ability to swerve, his lightness. So we need to add one more notion to our refinement of this quality, and that is to note the connection between lightness and grace.

Enlightenment

The problem of lightness seems a particularly contemporary theme. With billions of bits of information streaking every second through the air and over wires, with intercontinental travel now measured in fractions of days, our technologies seem to have acquired an enviable lightness and speed that we lack. For many adults, the experience of contemporary life is the opposite. Time pressures, stress, the accumulation of obligations, the miscellaneousness of information—these weigh us down and make life seem more laborious.

Sometimes, as William Wordsworth said in a moment of adult weariness, "the world is too much with us" and we feel weighed down by problems and responsibilities. Then humor comes to our rescue and "our spirits are lifted." Consider the physical experience of laughter: a sensation of shock and a sudden feeling of bodily weight being removed. Laughter comes in a lighten-ing stroke and is an en-lightening experience.

Robert Louis Stevenson, *Treasure Island* (1881; reprinted
Charles Scribner's Sons, 1911). Illustration by N. C. Wyeth.

George MacDonald, *The Light Princess*
(Farrar, Straus & Giroux, 1969). Illustration by
Maurice Sendak. © 1969 by Maurice Sendak.

But in mentioning the "weight" of the world (or "lightness" as a remedy), we should note that we are employing *physical* metaphors to describe metaphysical or existential experiences. Indeed, but especially for the child, there may be few other ways to discuss the otherwise invisible world of feelings and emotions. Even so, we should take note of this often unrecognized doubleness and the way the physical and the metaphysical are conflated.

Gravity, for example, is a word we use in two ways: as a term describing a physical property of Earth and as an expression referring to the trait of "seriousness." The conflation of these two is the basis of George MacDonald's brilliant and hilarious *The Light Princess*, where levity and levitation are counterposed.

MacDonald's children's story is easily told. Because a witch was not invited to the christening, she lays a curse on the baby that exempts the child from gravity. As a result, when the Light Princess is not held down, she bobs along the ceilings of rooms. The servants love to play ball (quite literally) with her, and the princess enjoys being outdoors when she is tethered and flown like a kite. Paralleling her physical circumstances are the princess's "high spirits." She lacks gravity in another fashion; she laughs all the time and fails to take anything seriously. A partial remedy comes halfway through the story; the maturing princess discovers that her gravity is restored when she is in water and swims in a lake (an experience she finds de-light-full). Toward the story's end she "falls" in love with a prince and her gravity is restored.

As even this description intimates, MacDonald's text is full of delicious doubleness and extended punning that conflates the physical and the metaphysical. At one point, for example, the princess's parents argue about her "infirmity," or lack of it:

[One day the king observed,] "It is a good thing to be light-hearted, I am sure, whether she be ours or not."

"It is a bad thing to be light-headed," answered the queen, looking with prophetic soul far into the future.

"'Tis a good thing to be light-handed," said the king.

"'Tis a bad thing to be light-fingered," answered the queen.

"'Tis a good thing to be light-footed," said the king.

"'Tis a bad thing—" began the queen; but the king interrupted her.

"In fact," said he, with the tone of one who concludes an argument in which he has had only imaginary opponents, and in which, therefore, he has come off triumphant—"in fact, it is a good thing altogether to be light-bodied."

"But it is a bad thing altogether to be light-minded," retorted the queen, who was beginning to lose her temper.

This last answer quite discomfited his Majesty, who turned on his heel, and betook himself to his counting-house again. But he was not half-way towards it, when the voice of his queen overtook him.

"And it's a bad thing to be light-haired," screamed she, determined to have more last words, now that her spirit was roused.

The queen's hair was black as night; and the king's had been, and his daughter's was, golden as morning. But it was not this reflection on his hair that arrested him; it was the double use of the word light. For the king hated all witticisms, and punning especially. And besides, he could not tell whether the queen meant light-haired or light-heired; for why might she not aspirate her vowels when she was ex-asperated herself?

MacDonald's story provides an occasion to examine humor as a way of evoking lightness. If gravity is a comprehensive form of determinism (not admitting of freedom, possibility, or spontaneity), then the role of the pun or double entendre in conversation is to evade weight—to introduce an awakened lightness into the midst of graveness, to offer a liberating antidote to the humdrum and the predictable, to offer a remedy to what we might call (to rephrase the title of Milan Kundera's book) The Unbearable Heaviness of the Boring. The witty riposte functions as an evasion of weight, a shift from seriousness, a failure to take seriously what others take seriously, and (when not entirely frivolous) an enlightened change of perspective meant to show others that they are mistakenly taking seriously what should not be taken seriously—confirming, in this way, the wisdom of Oscar Wilde's witticism that "life is too important to be taken seriously."

But evocations of lightness—and humor is one of these—are even more than evasions of weight or puckish redirection when "the world is too much with us." Behind images of lightness is also an endeavor to recover freedom, expand possibilities, and, ultimately, dissolve the solidity of the world.

The Polymorphous Worldview of Children

As Arthur Koestler suggests in *The Ghost in the Machine*, the great modern question proposed by traditional religion and conventional science is: Are we spirits or are we stones? Are we transient personalities or "messages" that inhabit matter, or are we separately existing and concrete objects in a world populated with similar entities? Today we might say: Are we software or are we hardware?

The latter may be the habitual way adults see themselves and the world, but the Party of Lightness means to undermine that. Images of lightness, in other words, are frequently associated with an alternate but familiar worldview. In childhood's aerial literature, the solidity of the world is dissolved and we are offered, instead, a universe of expanded possibility and remarkable plasticity.

This partially explains the popularity of that flying boy Harry Potter and his world of magic and wizards. Besides their preoccupation with flight, J. K. Rowling's books offer a vision of life where the solidity of this world has been dissolved and where transfiguration is common: a magical and fluid realm where an object or a person can easily morph into this shape and the next. This is not an uncommon worldview, we should note. Ovid in his *Metamorphoses*, for example, likewise presents such a vision of pervasive plasticity, of constant shape-shifting under the moon of gods and humans, trees and bulls, statues and stars.

In *Mary Poppins*, Pamela Travers also links the aerial with this worldview. Carrying her umbrella and blown by the wind, Mary Poppins arrives in a story full of images of lightness: when the nanny gracefully slides *up* the banister, when the children inflate with "laughing gas" and have a tea party on the ceiling, when a cow is obliged to go airborne and jump over the moon, when one of the Pleiades comes to visit and then returns to the sky, when Mary and her friends ascend ladders to paste stars back in the heavens. And these visions of lightness are entirely rooted in a particular worldview. The centerpiece of the book is the chapter "Full Moon," in which the children go to the zoo and Jane listens to the wise snake, the Hamadryad. His great message to Jane is this: "We are all made of the same stuff, remember, we of the Jungle, you of the City. The same substance composes us—the trees overhead, the stone beneath us, the bird, the beast, the star—we are all one, all moving to the same end. Remember that when you no longer remember me, my child."

The solidity of the world is dissolved in *Mary Poppins*. In place of our all too common and adult worldview of concrete and independently existing objects, Travers's Hamadryad offers an alternative: a vision of a single substance, taking this form and that and alive with possibility. Again, while an alternative, this worldview is familiar, and Travers's Hamadryad keeps company with Paramenides and with Heraclitus, with Buddha and with Ovid, with Lucretius and with recent theoretical scientists who see the world as a field of energy rather than a zone of solid matter.

Is there a reason, then, why this worldview and its accompanying visions of lightness should feature so prominently in Children's Literature? Child psychologist Jean Piaget has observed that youngsters, until they reach a certain point between the ages of nine and eleven, have an animistic view of the world. When they bump their knee on a table, they go back and strike the table. When a ball rolls, they are delighted and think it alive. When they play with the waves at the beach, the ocean seems to be teasing and playing tag with them. For them, the table, the ball, and the ocean are inhabited by spirits or by a *Spiritus Mundi* that engages them and from which they are not separate, disinterested parties. As the nursery rhyme has it, "I see the Moon, and the Moon sees me."

Of course, children are socialized out of this worldview and eventually come to see the world and themselves in a more conventional and consensual and adult way: as a concrete universe populated by separately existing and disinterested objects. And in a tradition at least as old as that of Rousseau's notion of the child, this socialization is sometimes regarded as a "fall." In *Mary Poppins*, for example, once they lose their baby teeth, the Banks twins are no longer able to understand what the sunlight says and what the chirping Starling is telling them. Likewise, in *Peter Pan*, the great tragedy of the conclusion is that Wendy, grown older, is no longer heartless and gay and can no longer fly. Images of flight and lightness in Children's Literature, in other words, appeal to the young because they confirm the worldview of childhood. In that sense, every adult is an Icarus who has grown older, acquired gravity, and suffered a fall.

There may, then, be three reasons that explain the unusual appeal and frequent appearance of images of flight and lightness in works written for children and enjoyed by them. First, images of lightness might be seen as an existential reaction to the weight or pressures of life and the world. Not surprisingly,

African American literature has its own tradition of flying stories represented in children's books like, for example, Virginia Hamilton's collection of folktales in *The People Could Fly*, her novel about her aerial hero *M. C. Higgins, the Great*, and Faith Ringgold's *Tar Beach*. Where men face "hard" facts, Hamlet's complaint seems apt: "O! That this too, too solid flesh would melt, thaw, and resolve itself into a dew." Where women are oppressed, witches fly. The same is the case with children: where needs are unmet, desires take wing.

Besides the existential explanation, there may also be a developmental one. Such images confirm a child's experience of the world before the fall, when the universe is an endless realm of seamless plasticity and a formless field of benefaction.

But there is still a third explanation, and that arises when we don't dismiss the unific worldview of childhood as naive animism but regard it, in fact, as another and valid way of seeing the world. Ovid and Buddha, Parmenides and Heraclitus, Pamela Travers and theoretical scientists, as well as countless others, have indicated that this may be so. We might agree as well. And as images of lightness suggest, when the metaphysical is mixed with the physical, when we are both spirits and stones, that experience of agreement is sometimes described as enlightenment.

Virginia Hamilton, *The People Could Fly* (Knopf, 2004).
Illustration by Leo and Diane Dillon.
© 2004 by Leo and Diane Dillon.

Carlo Collodi, *The Adventures of Pinocchio* (Running Press, 2003).
Illustration by Greg Hildebrandt. © 2003 by Greg Hildebrandt.

ALIVENESS 5

Laughter is prompted in the movie *Harvey* when a boozy adult (played by Jimmy Stewart) talks to an imaginary six-foot-high rabbit, but we hardly blink when Lewis Carroll's Alice converses with the White Rabbit in Wonderland. We aren't taken aback when animals talk in children's books because garrulous animals are commonplace. Creatures jabber away in Doctor Dolittle's world and trade insults in *The Jungle Books*. Black Beauty is one of many talking horses, Jack London's wolves loquacious, and Babar both an elephant and eloquent. We don't boggle when animals engage in conversation, as long as that happens in children's stories: the Ugly Duckling and the Frog Prince complaining about their treatment, a wolf threatening Little Red Riding Hood or the Three Little Pigs.

Needless to say, this isn't a common feature in adult stories. Norman Mailer isn't known for his talking animals, and John Updike's Rabbit novels (about that ordinary and contemporary adult named Rabbit Angstrom) aren't the same as accounts of Brer Rabbit or Peter Rabbit. We would be surprised if that were the case. But we aren't surprised, watching children's films, when Bambi or Dumbo or Nemo speaks; on the other hand, we might be stunned if the shark in *Jaws* was equally articulate. In the world of children's stories, all God's creatures seem chatty—whether they be bears, birds, cats, elephants, bugs, lions, pigs, dogs, monkeys, or fish in the sea.

We aren't surprised by talking animals in children's books because they feel and think like we do; there is no shock that might come from a more naturalistic presentation of their differences. In fact, the talking animals of children's stories so resemble us, they sometimes seem to be mocking us with their impersonations. The cartoon creatures that appear in animated films—from fussy elephants in Disney's *Dumbo* to hepcat monkeys in *The Jungle Book* and timid fish in *Nemo*—seem personality types we immediately recognize.

Take Badger in Kenneth Grahame's *The Wind in the Willows*. Everyone recognizes his type: that kind of peremptory and elderly gentleman who has made up his own mind about things

and can't be bothered with ceremony, that sort of sham cur-
mudgeon whose no-nonsense brusqueness scarcely conceals
his kindliness and heart of gold. As C. S. Lewis observes, "The
child who has once met Mr. Badger" has met an English type
and "has ever afterwards, in his bones, a knowledge of English
social history which he could not get in any other way."

Animals, by means of their analogies, represent the familiar
in other ways as well. Take Aesop. "The Story of the Ant and
the Grasshopper" is well known: how the ant is busily indus-
trious during the summer, storing up food against the winter,
and how the grasshopper fiddles away his time with no thought
of the future. Then comes the winter and the grasshopper begs
for food from the ant, but the ant turns him away with a lecture
about his being foolish during the summer.

That, more or less, is the whole of the story, but what has to
be remembered is that the morals that have now come to
accompany Aesop's fables were added hundreds of years later.
Nowadays, the lesson of this story, children are told, is that one
should be wise like the ant and plan for the future. But we
might just as easily draw another, more laissez-faire lesson: all
work and no play makes one as righteous and selfish as the ant.
In any event, Aesop's original fables give no clue about which
morals should be drawn. Aesop just tells the story and leaves

the listener to draw any conclusion. Aesop gives a snapshot of a familiar situation, a kind of "odd couple," a clash of two different sorts of personalities that we know and have seen a hundred times in a hundred different ways. Aesop makes clear a type of situation, and he does this by making use of animals. In their otherness but especially in their likeness, "animals are good to think with," Claude Lévi-Strauss observed.

Talking Animals

When animals talk in children's books, the young become accomplices in a remarkable extension of sympathy and compassion. In what Anna Sewell presents as the autobiography of a horse, Black Beauty speaks and movingly argues for more humane treatment of her kind. Doctor Dolittle may be remembered for his linguistic gifts but with these also comes the veterinarian's heightened concern for animals. Indeed, Hugh Lofting explained that the idea for the Dolittle books occurred to him when he reflected on the considerable role horses played in World War I:

They took their chances with the rest of us. But their fate was different from men's. However seriously a soldier was wounded . . . all the resources of surgery . . . were brought to his aid. [On the other hand,] a seriously wounded horse was put out by a timely bullet.

*In the evening, after dinner,
he tells the Old Lady's friends
all about his life in the great forest.—*

Jean de Brunhoff, *The Story of Babar, the Little Elephant,*
translated by Merle Haas (Random House, 1933).
© 1933, renewed 1961 by Random House, Inc.

This did not seem quite fair. If we made the animals take the same chances as we did ourselves, why did we not give them similar attention when wounded? But obviously to develop a horse-surgery as good as [surgical services for humans] would necessitate a knowledge of horse language.

That was the beginning of an idea: an eccentric country physician with a bent for natural history and a great love of pets, who finally decided to give up his human practice for the more difficult, more sincere and, for him, more attractive therapy of the animal kingdom.

As Lofting's use of the word *fair* suggests, underlying his books is an extensive egalitarianism where likeness is emphasized and otherness diminished.

When Doctor Dolittle begins to learn the languages of animals and converse with them, the question naturally arises why others haven't done so before. The answer the creatures offer is that humans have a smug sense of self-importance; "They think they're so wonderful," the old parrot Polynesia says. Out of this egotism arises a kind of dualistic thinking where humans reside within a circle of self-interest and self-importance, and on the other side of these self-erected barriers are those creatures now distantly regarded as "dumb" beasts.

Talking animals, however, call into question that dualistic thinking and that assertion of difference, and their frequent appearance in children's stories points to how the young think and see the world in a manner that varies from that of adults. In childhood, the ego is still in the process of being formed and has yet to be solidified. As a result, boundaries between the self and the non-self, between humans and animals, are fuzzier and less distinct.

Not yet fully socialized, the growing child has yet to embrace the adult notion that thinking and feeling are capabilities exclusive to us and our kind. Since children lack that sense of self-importance, in their nondualistic thinking, and as talking animals suggest, consciousness is permitted to exist or acknowledged to exist in the world at large.

Living Toys

It is one thing when familiar beasts of the air and creatures of the deep become loquacious, but it is another step altogether when consciousness is attributed to insentient things. In some children's stories, talking animals interact with talking toys: the evil Mouse King exchanges challenges with E. T. A. Hoffmann's wooden Nutcracker, the despotic Manny Rat discusses the meaning of life with a tin toy in Russell Hoban's *The Mouse and His Child*, and the wily Fox and Cat parlay with a puppet in Carlo Collodi's *Pinocchio*. Living toys present an even wider distribution of the attribute of consciousness and a more dramatic example of childhood's feelings of extended likeness.

Beatrix Potter, *The Tale of Two Bad Mice*
(Warne, 1904).

The presence of sentience in insentient things is neatly shown in Beatrix Potter's *The Tale of Two Bad Mice*. Destroying things here and there, these mice have made a mess of the nursery. When the little girl returns to that room, she carries her two dolls (Jane and Lucinda) with her. Potter writes: "What a sight met the eyes of Jane and Lucinda! Lucinda sat upon the stove and stared, and Jane leaned against the kitchen dresser and smiled; but neither of them made a remark."

In a stroke of genius that counterposes the sentient and the insentient, Potter pictures, on the opposite page, these dolls in dramatically rigid and sticklike postures. To say this differently, Potter's *picture* shows the dolls as any adult might see them: as sticklike, unmoving, and nonliving objects. But Potter's *words* (where Lucinda "stares" and Jane "smiles" at the mischief the mice have caused) speak about the dolls as a child sees them: not as objects but as living creatures with emotions, since the dolls are "stunned" or "amused" by the misbehavior of the mice. In short, these thinking and feeling toys are as alive as any human in the story, even though, as it happens, "neither of them made a remark."

A similar case of mute toys appears in "The Dumb Soldier," a poem in Robert Louis Stevenson's *A Child's Garden of Verses*. After the lawn is mown, a boy finds a hole in the turf and hides his tin soldier there; then comes the autumn and another mowing, and the toy is recovered. As the boy observes, the tin grenadier has witnessed much: seen the springing flowers and fairy things passing in the grass, heard the talking bee and ladybird, and more. But the Dumb Soldier is mute:

> Not a word will he disclose,
> Not a word of all he knows.
> I must lay him on the shelf,
> And make up the tale myself.

A too hasty understanding of the last line might suggest that, in "making up the tale," the boy is engaged in wholesale invention. Indeed, that might be described as the adult understanding of what is taking place in the poem. A conventional psychologist might see the boy's engagement with the toy as a classic example of "projection." A developmental psychologist might see here a specimen of that kind of immature thinking before a youngster has grasped the difference between living and nonliving things.

However, the poem itself suggests that the boy will have to make up the tale in the future but has yet to do so. More important, from the boy's point of view, the soldier would speak if he could—if he were not handicapped. The soldier's dumbness may be a disability, but that doesn't mean he isn't alive. Rather than a ventriloquist, in relating all the toy has seen (passing stars and fairies, talking bees and ladybirds, etc.), the child serves as interpreter or translator.

The aliveness of toys is important when the young play. Teddy bears engage in conversation. Toy soldiers do battle. Stick horses gallop. From the point of view of children, living toys actively participate in their lives and, as it were, from their side and at their own initiative. This is a way of thinking peculiar to childhood but not an unfamiliar one. Raise the subject at a cocktail party and some adults can still recall how, when they were young, they would check in the morning to see whether their dolls had moved overnight.

The Aliveness of Things

Dolls and toy soldiers, we might say, are predisposed to aliveness because, as semihuman objects, they are replicas. But it takes a much larger leap of faith to comprehend the child's attribution of consciousness to ordinary insentient things: to rocks and trees and Brave Little Toasters.

Moving things, of course, lend themselves more readily to the ascription of aliveness. In discussing Lightness, we have already noted how youngsters think that the rolling ball is alive and that the waves at the seashore are playing tag with them. In the same way, the child who watches dust motes twirling in a shaft of afternoon sunlight may also think these particles are alive—and no different, in that regard, from the atoms imagined by Lucretius: bits of matter, to be sure, but given to their own whimsy and swerves.

Motion separates a phenomenon from its background and gives it individuality. Consider how Mole, the childlike creature in *The Wind in the Willows*, regards such a moving thing when he sees a river for the first time:

Never in his life had he seen a river before—this sleek, sinuous, full-bodied animal, chasing and chuckling, gripping things with a gurgle and leaving them with a laugh, to fling itself on fresh playmates that shook themselves free, and were caught and held again. All was a-shake and a-shiver—glints and gleams and sparkles, rustle and swirl, chatter and bubble. The Mole sat bewitched, entranced, fascinated. By the side of the river he trotted as one trots, when very small, by the side of a man who holds one spellbound by exciting stories. . . . The river chattered on to him, a babbling procession of the best stories in the world.

Call it personification if you like, but a thing (albeit moving) is animal-like, alive, conscious, and companionable.

Stevenson takes up another dynamic phenomenon in his poem "The Wind," a song addressed by the child to its subject in a familiar way:

I saw you toss the kites on high
And blow the birds about the sky;
And all around I heard you pass,
Like ladies' skirts across the grass....

I saw the different things you did,
But always you yourself you hid.
I felt you push, I heard you call,
I could not see yourself at all....

O you that are so strong and cold,
O blower, are you young or old?
Are you a beast of field and tree,
Or just a stronger child than me?

Less solid a phenomenon than a river, invisible except in its effects, but still separable by the sensations and changes it causes, the Wind is like the child's waves at the seashore: a portion of the cosmos incarnate and dynamic; a companion that—or, better, *who*—enjoys playing hide-and-seek; a "you" with volition and personal habits of its own.

While undulating objects make easier the attribution of aliveness, it is quite another thing when an object is static and unchanging. Lying in a hospital bed in Paris, Ludwig Bemelmans's Madeline stares at the ceiling and notices a crack. She also notices that the crack "had a habit of looking like a rabbit."

If the question, then, is how far this childhood crediting and distribution of consciousness can go, Madeline's answer is that it can extend even to the static parts of the universe and *their* habits.

In the world of Children's Literature and in childhood, a cosmic urge to come alive seems operative everywhere. In the bit of slapstick that opens *Pinocchio*, a piece of wood loudly complains when a carpenter is about to strike it with an ax and then says it is being tickled when the man begins to plane the lumber. So the carpenter gives the piece of talking wood to his friend Geppetto, who starts to make a puppet: and when he has made a mouth, the puppet laughs at him; and when he has made hands, the puppet snatches Geppetto's wig; and when he makes feet, the puppet runs away. But that is not the end to this urge to awaken, since, as we know, this piece of wood wants to go further and become a real, live boy.

The wideness of the child's belief in consciousness in the world is also subtly evident in Margaret Wise Brown's *Goodnight Moon*. This beloved picture book begins with a child being put to bed and an itemization of both sentient and insentient things in "the great green room." In the second half, in a wide egalitarianism, each is bid goodnight: including kittens and mittens, clocks and socks, comb and brush, even a bowl full of

Ludwig Bemelmans, *Madeline* (Simon & Schuster, 1939).
© 1939, renewed 1967 by Madeline Bemelmans and
Barbara Bemelmans Marciano.

Randolph Caldecott, "The Dish Ran Away with the Spoon,"
in *Hey Diddle Diddle, and Bye, Baby Bunting* (Routledge, 1882).

mush—all these personable items being on an equal footing and deserving of a "goodnight."

We can more deeply understand this animation of insentient things by considering Badger's kitchen in *The Wind in the Willows*. In the words italicized below, Grahame particularly signals that the kitchen is a welcoming place:

The floor was well-worn red brick, and on the wide hearth burnt a fire of logs, between two attractive chimney-corners tucked away in the wall, well out of any suspicion of draught. A couple of high-backed settles, facing each other on either side of the fire, *gave* further sitting accommodations for the sociably disposed. In the middle of the room stood a long table of plain boards . . . [with] the remains of the Badger's plain but ample supper. Rows of spotless plates *winked* from the shelves of the dresser at the far end of the room, and from the rafters overhead hung hams, bundles of dried herbs, nets of onions, and baskets of eggs. It seemed a place where . . . two or three friends of simple tastes could sit about as they pleased and eat and smoke and talk in comfort and contentment. The ruddy brick floor *smiled* up at the smoky ceiling; the oaken settles, shiny with long wear, *exchanged* cheerful glances with each other; plates on the dresser *grinned* at pots on the shelf, and the *merry* firelight flickered and played over everything without distinction.

As Grahame's personifications suggest, Badger's kitchen is not simply a blank setting. This is a *living* place full of friendly, familiar objects; we might just as easily say that it is a happily haunted house full of friendly familiars. The smiling floor, the grinning plates, the merry fire—these are not just things but hybrids: conscious objects in a world where there is no distinct and dualistic boundary between fond feelings (on the one hand) and the objects' matter-of-factness (on the other). Rather, Badger's kitchen reveals a way of thinking where the two are intermingled. Like talking animals, like animated toys, with these alive things we encounter a conscious universe.

For the child, the world is a personable place: "I see the Moon, and the Moon sees me." And what is true of the Man in the Moon can also be said about the Sun and the face of the Clock and other capitalized phenomena. Even in the rough surfaces of a wall or in blobs of ink, the child can recognize faces of the polymorphous universe incarnating.

This same vision of cosmic plasticity and companionable incarnation is present in the familiar childhood phenomenon of the Imaginary Friend. Stevenson speaks of this in his poem "The Unseen Playmate":

> When children are playing alone on the green,
> In comes the playmate that never was seen.
> When children are happy and lonely and good,
> The Friend of the Children comes out of the wood.

Nobody heard him, and nobody saw,
His is a picture you never could draw,
But he's sure to be present, abroad or at home,
When children are happy and playing alone.

He lies in the laurels, he runs on the grass,
He sings when you tinkle the musical glass;
Whene'er you are happy and cannot tell why,
The Friend of the Children is sure to be by!

He loves to be little, he hates to be big,
'Tis he that inhabits the caves that you dig;
'Tis he when you play with your soldiers of tin
That sides with the Frenchmen and never can win.

'Tis he, when at night you go off to your bed,
Bids you go to sleep and not trouble your head;
For wherever they're lying, in cupboard or shelf,
'Tis he will take care of your playthings himself!

In this sense, the child is never alone in the world: a companion—or companions who come in thousands of shapes and forms—emerges out of the cosmos and incarnates.

The child's remarkable extension of consciousness, without check, to the whole universe is seen in Stevenson's poem "Night and Day," where he writes of a boy for whom the Whole World has gone away when he has fallen asleep and for whom the

Whole World awaits his waking up. At daybreak, there are birds singing, and shapes of things arising from the misty darkness that declare themselves to be houses, and dew upon the flowers in the garden. Then all these (birds, houses, dew, flowers)—and even such things as the path and the garden plot—have voices that call to him:

> Every path and every plot,
> Every blush of roses,
> Every blue forget-me-not
> Where the dew reposes,
>
> "Up!" they cry, "the day is come
> On the smiling valleys:
> We have beat the morning drum;
> Playmate, join your allies!"

Here is a vision of a conscious universe, both polymorphous and polyphonic.

Goodnight clocks
And goodnight socks

By Way of Conclusion

This wide distribution of consciousness is one of the most familiar features of children's thinking and is equally conspicuous in their literature. Of course, it would be foolish to romanticize that worldview and evangelically insist that the young's way of seeing the world is truer than our own. But it would be equally facile to take the high ground and smugly dismiss the ways the young think as mistaken and immature simply because they have yet to accept our own adult and no-nonsense worldview.

To be sure, in growing up, the gradual abandonment of childhood's notions of conscious things and of a conscious universe has its advantages. The eventual drawing of boundaries where they were absent and the acceptance of a consensual and dualistic point of view—where the sentient are divided from the insentient and humans from animals—are useful in a pragmatic way. When consciousness is seen to reside exclusively in us and the world apart from us is regarded as full of neutral and disinterested objects, the way is cleared for a less fettered pursuit of personal happiness. But—and this is a point important to grasp—the utility of the reductive worldview adults have settled upon is no guarantee of its veracity. It may simply be useful or expeditious in an existential way, in order to get ahead or get along in life.

In any event, the method of this book has been to set aside questions about the validity of worldviews. Studying the young, we have suspended disbelief and reserved judgment. Our endeavor has been to identify the ways the young think and see the world without labeling them "right" or "wrong," or even "cute" but "immature."

And the suggestion of this book has been that Children's Literature provides an especially good place for the study of childhood and the ways in which the young see the world. There we can glimpse and come to comprehend (or recall) what it feels like to be a kid: playing snugly under tables, shivering at scary stories, towering over small worlds, streaking lightly through earthbound life, and believing in talking animals and living toys.

In the introduction I suggested that Children's Literature provides a venue for these revelations because the great writers for children are still in touch with and can acutely recall their childhoods; this consciousness is the very source of these authors' popularity among young readers, their special ability to speak to the young where they are. Making that point, I mentioned having once asked Pamela Travers why her Mary

Poppins books appealed to the young and her having explained: "I have not forgotten my childhood. I can, as it were, turn aside and consult it."

Since the subject of this chapter has been the distribution of consciousness and the child's feeling that the world is alive, we might point to an example of this kind of recollection. Turning aside and consulting her childhood in just the way she described, Travers remembered her youthful conviction that the trees talked with each other but suddenly fell silent when she entered their grove. As Travers observed, there was only one thing for a young girl to do: "Be still long enough, I thought, and the trees would take no notice of me and continue whatever it was they were doing or saying before I happened upon them."

ACKNOWLEDGMENTS

A contention of this book is that children's authors differ from other kinds of writers in their ability to acutely recall their childhoods. In that regard, I must confess to also being one of those who can remember what it was like to play under tables or the danger at night of putting your foot over the edge of your bed because of the monsters that lived underneath; in response to the latter, I also recall the great assurance offered by my Irish-Catholic mother, who explained that my Guardian Angel would watch over me. Still, I owe a great debt to my children: being a parent to Breca and Colin has taught me much, both when they were young and when they grew older and could look back at their childhoods.

Of course, any university teacher writing a book of this kind must also acknowledge the valuable insights that come when one's ideas are tested in the give-and-take of the college classroom; in that vein, I wish to thank my students. Occasionally, some of my students accompanied me to elementary schools where we talked with—or, rather, listened to—first graders and fourth graders and where we learned that issues we teased from the depths of stories were close to the surface of children's lives; in that regard, I wish to thank the schoolteachers who welcomed us into their classrooms.

I also thank friends for their advice and encouragement: Linda Rodríguez, Michael Joseph, David Rudd, Lois Kuznets, Peter Neumeyer, Hamida Bosmajian, Alida Allison, June Cummins, Carole Scott, Philip Nel, Alison Lurie, John Seelye, Tom Wilson, Mary Galbraith, George Nicholson, Michael Cart, Gary Piepenbrink, Beverly Lyon Clark, Angelica Carpenter, Claire Green, and others. Finally, let me acknowledge San Diego State University for the provision of that kind of time which is money and for the special assistance of a Virginia R. and G. Pitt Warner Faculty Excellence Award.

Some of the work that appears here was first rehearsed in other publications—the *Los Angeles Times*, the Irish journal *Inis*, and *Parents' Choice*—and I am indebted to the editors who occasioned these forays. Functioning in a similar manner have been my editors Michael Lonegro and Linda Forlifer at the Johns Hopkins University Press and my indexer Lys Ann Weiss.

BIBLIOGRAPHY

Aesop. *Aesop's Fables*, ed. Jack Zipes (New York: Signet Classics, 2004).

Alcott, Louisa May. *Little Women* (New York: Penguin, 1997).

Allison, Alida, ed. *Russell Hoban / Forty Years: Essays on His Writing for Children* (New York: Garland, 2000).

Andersen, Hans Christian. *Andersen's Fairy Tales*, trans. Pat Shaw Iversen (New York: New American Library, 1987).

———. *Hans Andersen's Fairy Tales*, trans. Naomi Lewis (London: Penguin, 1981).

Ariès, Philippe. *Centuries of Childhood: A Social History of Family Life*, trans. Robert Baldick (New York: Random House, 1962).

Bachelard, Gaston. *The Poetics of Space*, trans. Maria Jolas (Boston: Beacon Press, 1969).

Barrie, J. M. *Peter Pan* (London: Penguin, 1994).

Baum, L. Frank. *The Wonderful Wizard of Oz* (New York: Dover, 1960).

Bemelmans, Ludwig. *Madeline* (New York: Penguin, 1978).

Bettelheim, Bruno. *The Uses of Enchantment* (New York: Random House, 1977).

Bharucha, Fershid, ed. *Buried Treasures: The Black-and-White Work of Max-field Parrish, 1896–1905* (San Francisco: Pomegranate, 1992).

Blount, Margaret. *Animal Land: The Creatures of Children's Fiction* (New York: Avon, 1977).

Bodanis, David. *The Secret House* (New York: Simon & Schuster, 1986).

Bosmajian, Hamida. "Vastness and Contraction of Space in *Little House on the Prairie*," *Children's Literature* 11 (1983): 49–63.

Brantley, Ben. "The Kiddie Show Goes Dark," *New York Times*, 1 May 2005.

Briggs, Raymond. *Fungus the Bogeyman* (New York: Penguin, 1990).

Brown, Margaret Wise. *Goodnight Moon*, illus. Clement Hurd (New York: Harper & Row, 1947).

Brown, Norman O. *Love's Body* (New York: Random House, 1966).

Burnett, Frances Hodgson. *The Secret Garden* (New York: HarperCollins, 1998).

Calvino, Italo. *Six Memos for the Next Millennium*, trans. Patrick Creagh (New York: Vintage, 1993).

———. *The Uses of Literature*, trans. Patrick Creagh (New York: Harcourt Brace, 1986).

Clark, Kenneth. *Looking at Pictures* (Boston: Beacon Press, 1968).

Coe, Richard N. *When the Grass Was Taller: Autobiography and the Experience of Childhood* (New Haven: Yale University Press, 1984).

Cohen, David, and Stephen A. MacKeith. *The Development of Imagination: The Private Worlds of Childhood* (London: Routledge, 1991).

Collodi, Carlo. *The Adventures of Pinocchio*, illus. Greg Hildebrandt (Philadelphia: Running Press, 2003).

———. *The Adventures of Pinocchio*, illus. Attilo Mussino, trans. Carol Della Chiesa (New York: Macmillan, 1926).

———. *Pinocchio*, trans. E. Harden (New York: Penguin, 1974).

Corentin, Philippe. *Papa!* (San Francisco: Chronicle Books, 1997).

Cott, Jonathan. *Pipers at the Gates of Dawn: The Wisdom of Children's Literature* (New York: Random House, 1983).

Coussens, Penrhyn W. *A Child's Book of Stories*, illus. Jesse Willcox Smith (New York: Diffield, 1911).

Dahl, Roald. *The BFG* (New York: Penguin, 1982).

Dalby, Richard. *The Golden Age of Children's Book Illustration* (London: Michael O'Mara Books, 1991).

De Brunhoff, Jean. *The Story of Babar, the Little Elephant*, trans. Merle S. Haas (New York: Random House, 1966).

De Brunhoff, Jean and Laurent. *Babar's Anniversary Album*, trans. Merle S. Haas (New York: Random House, 1981).

D'Erasmo, Stacey. "Little Grown-ups Live Here," *New York Times Magazine*, 2 October 2002, 100–103.

Dickens, Charles. *A Christmas Carol* (New York: Scholastic, no date).

Draper, Ellen Dooling, and Jenny Koralek, eds. *A Lively Oracle* (Lanham, Md.: Larson Publications, 1999).

Egoff, Sheila, G. T. Stubbs, and L. F. Ashley, eds. *Only Connect: Readings on Children's Literature* (Toronto: Oxford, 1980).

Erickson, Erik H. *Childhood and Society* (New York: Norton, 1993).

Grahame, Kenneth. *The Wind in the Willows*, illus. Michael Hague (New York: Holt, Rinehart & Winston, 1980).

———. *The Wind in the Willows*, illus. Arthur Rackham (New York: Knopf, 1993).

———. *The Wind in the Willows*, illus. Ernest Shephard (New York: Macmillan, 1989).

Grimm, Jacob and Wilhelm. *The Complete Fairy Tales of the Brothers Grimm*, trans. Jack Zipes (New York: Bantam, 1992), 2 vols.

Griswold, Jerry. *Audacious Kids: Coming of Age in America's Classic Children's Books* (New York: Oxford University Press, 1992). In revised paperback edition: *The Classic American Children's Story: Novels of the Golden Age* (New York: Penguin, 1996).

———. "Between Cultures: *Heidi* and *The Secret Garden*," *Teaching and Learning Literature*, March/April 1996, 26–29.

———. "Burdening Kids with Innocence," *Los Angeles Times*, 28 August 2002.

———. *The Children's Books of Randall Jarrell* (Athens: University of Georgia Press, 1988).

———. "Children's Literature in the USA: A Historical Overview," in *International Companion Encyclopedia of Children's Literature*, ed. Peter Hunt (London: Routledge, 2003), 1270–1279.

———. "The Disappearance of Children's Literature," in *Reflections of Change: Children's Literature since 1945*, ed. Sandra L. Becket (Westport, Conn.: Greenwood Press, 1997), 35–41.

———. "Fee Fi Ho Hum." *Los Angeles Times*, 28 October 2002.

———. Review of *Fly by Night*, by Randall Jarrell and pictures by Maurice Sendak, *New Republic* 176, nos. 1 and 2 (1977): 37–38.

———. "The Future of the Profession," *The Lion and the Unicorn* 26, no. 2 (2002): 236–242.

———. "Introduction" to *The Voyages of Doctor Dolittle*, by Hugh Lofting (New York: New American Library, 2000).

———. Review of *Kiddie Lit*, by Beverly Lyon Clark, *Children's Literature Association Quarterly* 28, no. 4 (Winter 2003–2004): 248–249.

———. *The Meanings of "Beauty and the Beast"* (Peterborough, Ontario: Broadview Press, 2004).

———. Review of *The Nutcracker*, by E. T. A. Hoffmann, trans. by Ralph

Manheim, pictures by Maurice Sendak, *Los Angeles Times Book Review*, 11 November 1984, 1, 6.

———. "The Original Ugly Duckling," review of *Hans Christian Andersen*, by Jens Andersen, *Los Angeles Times Book Review*, 3 April 2005, R9.

———. "Peter Rabbit Turns 100," *Los Angeles Times Book Review*, 15 August 1993, 11.

———. (with Edwina Burness). "P. L. Travers: The Art of Fiction LXIII," *Paris Review* 24, no. 85 (Winter 1982): 210–229. Reprinted in *Writers at Work*, Ninth Series, ed. George Plimpton (New York: Penguin, 1992), 37–53. Reprinted in *Women Writers at Work*, rev. ed., ed. George Plimpton (New York: Penguin, 1998).

———, ed. *The Prince and the Pauper*, by Mark Twain (New York: Penguin, 1997).

———. "Reading Differently after September 11," *Inis*, Autumn 2002, 6–7, 15.

———. "The Real Peter Pan," *Los Angeles Times Book Review*, 26 January 1992, 11.

———. "Revealing Herself to Herself" [a remembrance of P. L. Travers], *Los Angeles Times Book Review*, 16 June 1996, 2.

———. "Seuss, Sendak, Steig," review of *Pipers at the Gates of Dawn: The Wisdom of Children's Literature*, by Jonathan Cott, *Los Angeles Times Book Review*, 19 June 1983, 9.

———. "12 Representative American Children's Books," *Inis*, Summer 2003, 21–24.

———. (with Amy Wallace). "What Famous People Read," *Parade Magazine*, 13 March 1983, 21–25.

———. Review of *When the Grass Was Taller: Autobiography and the Experience of Childhood*, by Richard Coe, *Los Angeles Times Book Review*, 20 January 1985, 3.

Hamilton, Virginia. *M. C. Higgins, the Great* (New York: Macmillan, 1974).

———. *The People Could Fly*, illus. Leo and Diane Dillon (New York: Knopf, 2004).

Hoban, Russell. *The Mouse and His Child* (New York: Harper & Row, 1967).

Hoffmann, E. T. A. *Nutcracker*, trans. Ralph Mannheim, illus. Maurice Sendak (New York: Crown, 1984).

———. *The Nutcracker and the Golden Pot*, ed. Philip Smith, various translators (New York: Dover, 1993).

Hoffmann, Heinrich. *Der Struwwelpeter* (Erlangen, Germany: Pestalozzi-Verlag, 1998).

———. *Struwwelpeter*, introduction by Jack Zipes (Venice, Calif.: Feral House, 1999).

Hunt, Caroline C. "Dwarf, Small World, Shrinking Child: Three Versions of the Miniature," *Children's Literature* 23 (1995): 115–136.

Hurlimann, Bettina. *Three Centuries of Children's Books in Europe*, trans. Brian W. Alderson (New York: World Publishing, 1967).

Jarrell, Randall. *The Animal Family*, pictures by Maurice Sendak (New York: Dell, 1984).

———. *The Collected Poems* (New York: Noonday Press, 1981).

———. *Fly by Night*, illus. Maurice Sendak (New York: Farrar, Straus & Giroux, 1976).

Jones, Gerard. *Killing Monsters* (New York: Basic, 2002).

Kingsley, Charles. *The Water Babies* (New York: Penguin, 1995).

Kipling, Rudyard. *The Jungle Books* (New York: New American Library, 1961).

Klause, Anette Curtis. "The Lure of Horror," *School Library Journal* 43, no. 11 (November 1997): 38.

Koestler, Arthur. *The Ghost in the Machine* (London: Hutchinson, 1976).

Kuznets, Lois R. *Kenneth Grahame* (Boston: Twayne, 1987).

———. *When Toys Come Alive* (New Haven: Yale University Press, 1994).

Lane, Margaret. *The Tale of Beatrix Potter* (New York: Penguin, 1986).

Lanes, Selma. *The Art of Maurice Sendak* (New York: Abrams, 1984).

Lewis, C. S. "On Three Ways of Writing for Children," in *Only Connect: Readings on Children's Literature*, ed. Sheila Egoff, G. T. Stubbs, and L. F. Ashley (Toronto: Oxford University Press, 1980).

Lofting, Hugh. *The Story of Doctor Dolittle* (New York: Dell, 1988).

———. *The Voyages of Doctor Dolittle* (New York: New American Library, 2000).

London, Jack. *White Fang and the Call of the Wild* (New York: Penguin, 1994).

Lurie, Alison. *Boys and Girls Forever* (New York: Penguin, 2003).

———. *Don't Tell the Grown-ups* (Boston: Little Brown, 1990).

MacDonald, George. *The Light Princess*, illus. Maurice Sendak (New York: Dell, 1969).

Maguire, Gregory. "Belling the Cat: Heroism and the Little Hero," *Lion and the Unicorn* 13, no. 1 (1989): 102–119.

Manguel, Alberto, and Gianni Guadalupi. *The Dictionary of Imaginary Places* (New York: Macmillan, 1980).

Marcus, Leonard. *Margaret Wise Brown: Awakened by the Moon* (New York: William Morrow, 1999).

Masefield, John. *Grace before Ploughing* (London: William Heinemann, 1966).

Mayer, Mercer. *There's a Nightmare in My Closet* (New York: Penguin, 1976).

Moore, Clement C. *The Night before Christmas*, illus. James Marshall (New York: Scholastic, 1985).

Morris, Jan. *The Matter of Wales* (New York: Oxford, 2005).

Nikolajeva, Maria, and Carole Scott. *How Picturebooks Work* (New York: Garland, 2001).

Nodelman, Perry. *Words about Pictures* (Athens: University of Georgia, 1988).

Norton, Mary. *The Borrowers: Fiftieth Anniversary Gift Edition*, illus. Diana Stanley (New York: Harcourt, 2003).

O'Neil, Dennis. *Secret Origins of the Super DC Heroes* (New York: Harmony, 1976).

Pascal. *Pensées*, trans. A. J. Krailsheimer (New York: Penguin, 1995).

Perrault, Charles. *Perrault's Fairy Tales*, trans. A. E. Johnson, illus. Gustave Doré (New York: Dover, 1969).

Peter Pan's A B C, illus. Flora White (Hodder & Stoughton, n.d. [ca. 1914]).

Piaget, Jean. *The Child's Concept of the World* (New York: Harcourt Brace, 1929).

———. *The Construction of Reality in the Child* (New York: Basic, 1954).

———. *The Origins of Intelligence in Children* (New York: International Universities Press, 1952).

Potter, Beatrix. *Beatrix Potter: The Complete Tales. The Twenty-three Original Peter Rabbit Books and Four Unpublished Works* (New York: Frederick Warne, 1997).

———. *The Tailor of Gloucester* (New York: Dover, 1973).

———. *The Tale of Peter Rabbit* (New York: Dover, 1972).

———. *The Tale of Two Bad Mice* (New York: Dover, 1974).

Ratcliff, Carter. *John Singer Sargent* (New York: Abbeville, 1982).

Ringgold, Faith. *Tar Beach* (New York: Crown Publishers, 1991).

Roalf, Peggy. *Looking at Paintings: Families* (New York: Hyperion, 1992).

Rowling, J. K. *Harry Potter and the Philosopher's Stone* (London: Bloomsbury, 1997).

Santayana, George. *Scepticism and Animal Faith* (New York: Dover, 1955).

Scarry, Elaine. *Reading by the Book* (New York: Farrar, Straus & Giroux, 1999).

Sendak, Maurice. *Caldecott & Co.* (New York: Farrar, Straus & Giroux, 1988).

———. *Where the Wild Things Are* (New York: Harper & Row, 1963).

Seuss, Dr. (pseud. Theodor Geisel). *The Cat in the Hat* (New York: Random House, 1957).

———. *How the Grinch Stole Christmas* (New York: Random House, 1957).

Sewell, Anna. *Black Beauty* (Hertfordshire, U.K.: Wordsworth, 1993).

Siegel, Muffy. "Like: The Discourse Particle and Semantics," *Journal of Semantics* 19, no. 1 (February 2002): 35–71.

Spyri, Johanna. *Heidi*, trans. Eileen Hall (New York: Penguin, 1984).

———. *Heidi*, illus. Gustaf Tenggren (Boston: Houghton Mifflin, 1923).

———. *Heidi*, illus. Jesse Wilcox Smith (New York: HarperCollins, 1996).

Stallcup, Jackie. "Power, Fear, and Children's Picture Books," *Children's Literature* 30 (2002): 125–158.

Steig, William. *Sylvester and the Magic Pebble* (New York: Simon & Schuster, 1980).

Stevens, Wallace. *The Collected Poems of Wallace Stevens* (New York: Knopf, 1968).

Stevenson, Robert Louis. *A Child's Garden of Verses* (New York: Dover, no date).

———. *Treasure Island* (New York: Penguin, 1984).

———. *Treasure Island*, illus. N. C. Wyeth (New York: Atheneum, 2003).

Swift, Jonathan. *Gulliver's Travels* (New York: Penguin, 2003).

Tatar, Maria, ed. *The Annotated Classic Fairy Tales* (New York: Norton, 2002).

———. *The Classic Fairy Tales* (New York: Norton, 1999).

Thomas, Bob. *Disney's Art of Animation* (New York: Hyperion, 1991).

Travers, P. L. *Mary Poppins*, rev. ed., illus. Mary Shepard (New York: Harcourt Brace, 1981).

———. *What the Bee Knows* (London: Penguin, 1993).

Twain, Mark. *The Adventures of Tom Sawyer* (New York: Penguin, 1986).

Van Allsburgh, Chris. *The Garden of Abdul Gasazi* (Boston: Houghton Mifflin, 1979).

Warner, Marina. *No Go the Bogeyman* (New York: Farrar, Straus & Giroux, 1998).

Weil, Simone. *Gravity and Grace*, trans. Emma Crauford (London: Routledge, 1963).

White, E. B. *The Annotated Charlotte's Web*, ed. Peter Neumeyer (New York: HarperCollins, 1994).

———. *Charlotte's Web*, illus. Garth Williams (New York: HarperCollins, 1980).

———. *Stuart Little*, illus. Garth Williams (New York: Harper & Row, 1945).

Wilder, Laura Ingalls. *Little House on the Prairie* (New York: Harper & Row, 1971).

Zipes, Jack. *Sticks and Stones* (New York: Routledge, 2002).

———. *The Trials and Tribulations of Little Red Riding Hood* (New York: Routledge, 1993).

INDEX